The American Dream
vs.
The Gospel of Wealth

With all good wishes

The American Dream

vs

The Gospel of Wealth

The Fight for a Productive Middle-Class Economy

NORTON GARFINKLE

Yale University Press   New Haven and London

Published with assistance from the Mary Cady Tew Memorial Fund.

The Future of American Democracy series aims to examine, sustain, and renew the historic vision of American democracy in a series of books by some of America's foremost thinkers. The books in the series present a new, balanced, centrist approach to examining the challenges American democracy has faced in the past and must overcome in the years ahead.

Series editor: Norton Garfinkle.

Library of Congress Cataloging-in-Publication Data
Garfinkle, Norton, 1931–
The American dream vs. the gospel of wealth : the fight for a productive middle-class economy / Norton Garfinkle.
p. cm. — (Future of American democracy series)
Includes bibliographical references and index.
ISBN-13: 978-0-300-10860-6 (alk. paper)
ISBN-10: 0-300-10860-5 (alk. paper)
1.   United States—Economic conditions.   2. United States—Economic policy.   3. Middle class—United States.   4. Supply-side economics—United States.   5. Democracy—United States.   I. Title.   II. Series: Future of American democracy.
HC103.G32 2006
330.973—dc22   2006013529

A catalogue record for this book is available from the British Library.

The paper in this book meets the guidelines for permanence and durability of the Committee on Production Guidelines for Book Longevity of the Council on Library Resources.

10 9 8 7 6 5 4 3 2 1

Contents

Preface

Americans today confront a choice between two fundamentally different economic visions for America. The historic vision of the American Dream is that continuing economic growth and political stability can be achieved by supporting income growth and economic security of middle-class families without restricting the ability of successful businessmen to gain wealth. The counterbelief, based on the Gospel of Wealth, is that providing maximum financial rewards to the most successful businessmen is the way to maintain high economic growth to benefit all Americans. Both visions claim to support the goals of maximum economic growth and maximum benefit for the society as a whole, but they present radically divergent programs to achieve these goals. One approach claims that the engine of economic growth can best be sustained by a progressive tax system that supports the purchasing power of middle-class Americans. The other claims that the engine of economic growth can best be sustained by a regressive tax system that increases the wealth of the highest income families to support business investment. This book draws on the historic record and a detailed analysis of economic data to demonstrate that the middle-class American Dream not only supports the democratic ideals of our society but also provides the best path to maximum economic growth.

The American Dream vs. The Gospel of Wealth is a volume in the Yale University Press Series on the Future of American Democracy. Yale University Press has joined with the Yale Center for International and Area Studies and The Future of American Democracy Foundation to sponsor this series of books by some of America's foremost thinkers. These books, together with articles, lectures, conferences, and television programs, are designed to stimulate historically informed analysis of contemporary public policy issues and to help Americans build a shared, sensible, and positive vision of the future of our democratic society.

The Future of American Democracy Foundation is a nonprofit, nonpartisan foundation dedicated to research and education aimed at renewing and sustaining the vision of American democracy that has unified Americans throughout the nation's history. The goal of the Foundation is to clarify the domestic and foreign policy choices facing the United States in the years ahead. A distinguished group of scholars and experts serves as the Foundation's officers and as members of the Foundation's Board of Advisors, including Jonathan Brent (Editorial Director of Yale University Press), John Donatich (Director, Yale University Press), Fredrica S. Friedman (President of Fredrica S. Friedman & Co., Inc.), Norton Garfinkle (Chair of the Foundation), William R. Griffith (Reed Smith LLP), Richard D. Heffner (Host, "The Open Mind"), Thomas E. Mann (The Brookings Institution), Norman Ornstein (American Enterprise Institute), Hugh Price (Former President of the National Urban League), Jeffrey Rosen (George Washington University), Ian Shapiro (Sterling Professor and Director of the Yale Center for International and Area Studies), Alan Wolfe (Boston College),

Ruth A. Wooden (President, Public Agenda) and Daniel Yankel-ovich (Chairman, Public Agenda). Please visit www.futureof americandemocracyfoundation.org for the latest information on the Foundation's activities.

I would like to thank my colleagues Daniel Yankelovich, Richard Heffner, Ian Shapiro, and my wife, Sally Minard, for their sage advice on the substance of this book. Shivaun McDonagh worked tirelessly to create the final manuscript. Our agent, Fredrica Friedman, a consummate publishing professional, made a major contribution to the success of this volume. And finally I want to express my gratitude to Jonathan Brent, Sarah Miller, and their excellent editorial and production team at Yale University Press for a superb job in bringing this book to the public.

Introduction

As the new millennium dawned in 2000, the American economy presented an extraordinary portrait of success. For the previous four years, Gross Domestic Product (GDP) had grown at an average real rate of 4.2 percent, a figure well above the 3.2 percent average for the post–World War II era. Unemployment, at 4.2 percent, was well below the postwar average. Inflation was minimal. Yearly growth in business investment was at levels not seen since the 1960s. Indeed, to find a similar run of robust economic growth, low unemployment, low inflation, and high business investment, one would have to go back to the mid-1960s—and back then, inflation was showing signs of increasing. To top it off, by the end of 2000, the federal government had produced surpluses for three consecutive years—a minor miracle, not seen since the late 1940s. Moreover, federal surpluses in the multibillions were projected as far as the eye could see. From 1993 through 2000, the U.S. economy created over 23 million new jobs, an average of more than 2.9 million a year.[1] Americans were enjoying an unprecedented level of prosperity. Government's fiscal house was in order. The federal government was not only able to pay down trillions in accumulated debt; it had money left over to help cope with looming crises in Social Security and Medicare.

But all this was to end.

First came the inevitable. In March 2000, an inflated technology stock market crashed, setting the stage for the onset of a recession a year later. Then came the policymakers. President George W. Bush came to office in 2001 with a minority of the popular vote, a razor-thin electoral vote margin, and a radical plan to slash federal taxes. Tax cuts, the president and his advisers said, were the key to increasing investment. Tax cuts were the key to increasing jobs. Tax cuts were the key to getting the economy back on a pathway of growth. Between 2001 and 2003, the Bush administration pushed through major cuts in the income tax, the estate tax, corporate taxes, and taxes on dividends and capital gains. By 2004, the administration's tax cuts had trimmed over $200 billion from the federal government's annual revenues, with most of the money going to those in the top 12 percent of the income scale.[2]

Yet the results were not what the president and his advisers predicted. First to disappear were the projected federal surpluses. From a surplus of $256 billion in 2000, the federal budget went to a deficit of $413 billion in fiscal year 2004 and $319 billion in 2005. The number of new jobs created fell far short of economists' estimates of the minimum of 150,000 per month needed to accommodate new entrants to the labor force. Indeed in the five years of the Bush administration from 2001 to 2005, the economy created only 31,000 new jobs per month compared to 240,000 per month during the eight years of President Bill Clinton's administration. The promised business investment boom was slow to materialize. Business investment growth during the first five years of the Bush administration averaged only 1.2 percent per year compared to 9.9 percent per year during the Clinton presidency. From the combined standpoint of employment, business investment, and real GDP growth, the Bush administration presided over one of the slowest recoveries of the post–World War II era. During these five years of the Bush administration the average annual GDP growth of 2.6 percent was considerably lower than the average annual growth of 3.7 percent during the eight Clinton years. Annual employment growth was anemic at 0.3 percent compared to 2.4 percent during the Clinton years. And even in 2005, three years into the recovery, GDP growth was only 3.5 percent and employment growth remained anemic at 1.5 percent.[3]

After five years of their ambitious tax-cutting program, in other words, the central claim of President Bush and his advisers—that tax cuts would create a fundamentally new economic environment that fostered historically high rates of investment, job creation, and growth—had not panned out. At the same time, having added nearly $2.3 trillion to the national debt in the brief span of five years, the administration was still confronted with an array of urgent spending requirements— billions for homeland security following the terrorist attacks of September 11, 2001, a protracted and costly military occupation of Iraq, substantial relief and reconstruction costs after Hurricanes Katrina and Rita, and burgeoning oil prices—all destined to take their continuing toll on both the federal budget and the U.S. economy.

The crowning irony was that the sustained boom of the 1990s had been ushered in by a major *tax increase* during the Clinton administration while the Bush *tax cuts* produced nothing of the kind.

What rationale could the Bush administration have had

for wreaking such havoc on the federal finances? Why insist on deep tax cuts, especially in the post–September 11 era, when security spending was bound to explode and costly disasters awaited right around the corner? How would major tax breaks for the highest-income earners work magic on an economy that had already been growing for several years at faster-than-historical rates—under a progressive tax structure that produced healthy federal surpluses? Why was the Bush administration content to throw away federal surpluses when huge unfunded liabilities for Social Security and Medicare loomed on the horizon, to say nothing of a dizzying array of immediate security, defense, and disaster needs?

The answer lay in the doctrine of supply-side economics, which thoroughly permeated the thinking of Bush and his economic advisers. Supply-side economics was the conservative answer to the demand-side economics that dominated U.S. policymaking from the end of World War II until 1980. To a large degree, economic debate in America for the past quarter century has centered on the conflict between these two economic visions. The health of both our economy and our democracy will be decisively affected by which of these two visions prevails in the future.

Drawing on historical analysis and data-based research, this book shows how Americans today confront a choice between two fundamentally different economic visions for American society, each of which claims to support maximum economic growth and a fair and equitable basis for American democratic society. One vision, based on the American Dream, supports a progressive tax structure that enables the government to implement programs to strengthen the income and economic security of the middle class and ordinary wage earners without restricting the ability of successful businessmen to gain wealth. The second vision, based on the Gospel of Wealth, seeks to ensure that the few most economically successful citizens reap maximum rewards through an increasingly regressive tax structure.

The data analyzed in this book clearly indicate that regressive tax policies based on a Gospel of Wealth supply-side theory are not helpful to economic growth, while progressive tax policies based on demand-side theory can provide a continuing spur to economic growth consistent with the economic and political vision of the American Dream.

Two Theories, Three Questions

Every important economic policy has three kinds of consequences: factual, moral, and political. In effect, in evaluating economic policy, we have to ask three questions: (1) Does it work? (2) Is it fair? and (3) Will it sustain the democratic structure of our society?

Today our debate tends to focus almost exclusively on the first question, at the expense of the other two. It was not always so. A generation ago, most Americans would have instinctively understood the relevance of all three questions—factual, moral, and political. That is because public views of government economic policy were shaped by memories of the Great Depression. The Great Depression brought dramatic policy failure on all three levels. When the economy nosedived after the Great Stock Market Crash of 1929, the federal government literally did not know what to do. By and large, the federal government stood by almost helplessly as unemployment rose to catastrophic levels, eventually as high as 25 percent. Some of the steps the government took, including a tax increase in 1932, actually made conditions worse. Perhaps most gallingly, the otherwise compassionate president Herbert Hoover adamantly opposed any federal spending for relief of the millions of unemployed. It is hard for Americans today to imagine unemployment at such levels, or what unemployment could be like in the absence of any federal unemployment insurance program. Millions of Americans were literally homeless and starving. Men rode the rails from town to town in vain search of employment. Hundreds of thousands of families, ejected from homes and apartments for which they could no longer pay mortgages or rent, lived in camps of tents and shanties that popped up in vacant lots of major cities—popularly called Hoovervilles. Most Americans became convinced of three things: that the government under Hoover did not know what it was doing, that the fate meted out to ordinary workers and their families was patently unfair, and that unemployment and spreading poverty threatened the very basis of American democracy.

After the economy recovered in World War II, Americans were still thinking within this framework. Demand-side economics, which became a kind of unofficial economic policy for the nation in the postwar years, reflected this understanding. It integrated technical economic insights developed by the British economist John Maynard Keynes with the moral and political imperatives that had grown out of the Great Depression. In a book written in 1936, Keynes showed policymakers a way out of the Depression. Keynes's key innovation was to shift the focus of economists from production, or supply, as the engine of economic growth to the importance of consumption, or demand. The main lesson economists drew from Keynes was that government could restore growth to an economy suffering from high unemployment by engaging in deficit spending to expand "aggregate demand." Expanded demand would get the economy moving again, provide customers for business, give investors a reason to invest, and bring down unemployment.

By the beginning of President Dwight Eisenhower's administration in 1953, demand-side economics had become the basis for a bipartisan consensus. The post–World War II economy was understood to be "Everyman's economy." By broad social consensus, the purpose of the economy was to provide economic opportunities as well as a measure of economic security for ordinary workers and their families. Government was understood to have an active role—indeed, a responsibility—in this process.

The demand-side consensus constituted the basis of an economy that saw a remarkable growth of the American middle class. It was an economy in which ordinary workers in ordinary jobs could expect to better their conditions, own homes and automobiles, send their children to college, and retire in relative security. It was an economy in which the vast majority of citizens had a stake. It was an economy that promoted a strong faith in democracy.

Beginning in the mid-1960s, however, the demand-side consensus began to go awry. President Lyndon Johnson embarked simultaneously on massive federal spending to pay for a rash of Great Society antipoverty programs and equally massive spending to pay for the Vietnam War. The resulting huge expansion in the federal deficit (combined with the president's pressure on the Federal Reserve to keep money "easy") resulted in the emergence of high inflation. For roughly fifteen years, inflation remained a problem that would not go away. As inflation grew, the only alternative seemed to be restrictive policies that would create high unemployment—but preventing unemployment was the central goal of demand-side economics. By the 1970s, the economy began to experience "stagflation"—high inflation together with high unemployment. For middle-class Americans, stagflation represented the worst economic crisis since the Great Depression. Prices became unpredictable.

Raises in salaries and wages were eaten up by price increases. Savings eroded as the value of money declined. Mortgage interest rates went through the roof. Moreover, Americans experienced ever-higher taxes as inflation drove them into higher and higher income tax brackets, brackets originally intended for the very rich.

Supply-side economics arose in direct reaction to the inflation crisis. The architects of supply-side economics—most of them political commentators rather than trained economists—created, in effect, a mirror image of demand-side theory. The real engine of growth in an economy was not demand, said the supply-siders, but rather supply. The problem was that the government was pumping too much demand into the economy via its deficits, while its high taxes were inhibiting supply, by killing off economic "incentives" to produce. Taxes were too high to encourage investors to invest. Fewer products and services were being generated. Demand therefore had nowhere to go, which is why inflation was so high. Only the private sector could generate economic growth, and the private sector needed to be set free to do its job. Supply-siders saw tax cuts—and especially tax cuts for the highest-income taxpayers—as the key to generating new investment and production and, so they argued, eliminating inflation.

Supply-siders believed that demand-siders had put too much emphasis on the issue of fairness and in the process they had neglected job 1—which was to make the economy grow. One could engineer fairness, the supply-siders believed, only at the expense of economic growth. The government had been trying too hard to control the economy; now the government had to learn to obey the laws of economics. If the laws of economics brought lower wages or greater income inequality, so be it. The important thing was to ensure growth. That meant getting government out of the way. Government should not be worrying about how economic goods were being distributed; it should not be worrying about ensuring an Everyman's economy or building up the middle class. It should simply get its hands off business and the economy and let business and the economy generate growth. The most important way for government to get its hands off the economy was to lower taxes, especially on the highest earners, the most productive citizens who would invest their increased revenue in their own businesses. Many supply-siders claimed that such tax cuts would so powerfully unleash the forces of supply that the tax cuts would not even produce a deficit: they would pay for themselves.

The Republican candidate Ronald Reagan made supply-side tax cuts the center of his presidential campaign in 1980, and once in office President Reagan implemented the supply-side program full-bore, pushing through the largest tax cut in history, including a deep reduction in the top marginal income tax rate—eventually cutting the top rate down from 70 percent to 28 percent.[4]

By the end of the Reagan administration, however, few mainstream economists regarded the supply-side tax cut "experiment" as a success. In the first place, the tax cuts had obviously not "paid for themselves" (almost no mainstream economist expected they would). The Reagan administration's taxing and spending policies produced the largest peacetime federal deficits in American history. Nor did the cuts in taxes for the highest-income earners bring the promised investment boom. In the seven years following the 1981 *tax cut* (1982–88), growth in new business investment averaged a weak 3.1 percent. Compare that to the 10.1 percent average growth in new business investment in the seven years following the Clinton administration's 1993 *tax increase* (1994–2000).[5] To be sure, the economy

showed healthy growth during the later Reagan years. But economists generally agree that the recovery was primarily a result of
gaining control over inflation. This had nothing to do with tax
cuts (indeed, the tax cuts aggravated the situation by con-
tributing to large deficits). Rather, the recovery was mostly the
result of a decisive shift toward a more disciplined monetary
policy by the Federal Reserve.

It was one thing for supply-siders to claim to emphasize
the factual dimension of economic issues at the expense of the
moral and the political questions. That was simply a debating
posture. It was another thing to actually have a factual basis
for their claims (see chapter 8). Absent such factual support, it
is interesting to ask why supply-side economics made such a
powerful comeback under President George W. Bush.

Today we are at a crossroads. Not only has the supply-
side program failed to deliver the promised higher levels of investment and faster-than-historical rates of economic growth.
It has once again produced outsized deficits. It has intensified
already burgeoning income inequality. And it has gone hand in
hand with an economy that year after year has brought slug-
gish employment growth, stagnant wages, increasing job insecurity, and millions of citizens slipping below the poverty line.
The federal government is in debt up to its ears, and so are many
Americans, as ordinary citizens max out their credit cards and
borrow against their home equity in a desperate effort to maintain a middle-class standard of living in an economy apparently no longer defined by a commitment to support such a
living standard.

The word "economics" comes from a Greek term meaning "household management." But economics in America has
always been about more than managing the national household.

It has always been about more than dollars and cents. It has been about defining who we are, and what kind of a nation we seek to be. The promise of the American economy and the promise of America itself have always been closely bound up together. What kind of an economy do we seek, and what kind of a nation do we wish to be? Do we want to be the kind of country in which, as an old song from the 1920s went, "The rich get rich, and the poor get poorer"? Or do we want to be the kind of country we set out to be at the end of World War II, committed to an economy that provides for the common good, offers ready entry to the middle class, supports a middle-class standard of living, and provides generous opportunities for all? When the richest nation in the world has to borrow hundreds of billions to pay its bills, when its middle-class citizens sit on a mountain of debt to maintain their living standard, when the nation's economy has difficulty producing secure jobs or enough jobs of any kind, something is amiss.

This book is an effort to illuminate the road ahead in economic policy by using the historical record to clarify not only the factual consequences of alternative policy choices but also the moral and political consequences of these choices. Only by understanding all three dimensions can we sustain our historic commitment to a productive economy, guided by principles of fairness, that helps sustain the middle-class basis of our political democracy.

Can we regain our political, moral, and economic compass? To recover it we need to go back to the beginning and ask what kind of nation and what kind of economy America was intended to be.

Chapter I
The American Economic Vision

I s there an American economic vision? Is there some guiding principle of economics implicit in our Declaration of Independence, our Constitution, and our form of government? There is—though at first glance this principle might appear to have little to do with the modern debates over fiscal and monetary policy, the size of government, or the degree of government regulation of economic life. But underlying these modern debates is an economic vision familiar to virtually all Americans: the American Dream—the dream that all Americans will have the opportunity through hard work to build a comfortable middle-class life.

To a large degree, the history of American economic policy making is the story of the waxing and waning of this middle-class ideal. When Alexis de Tocqueville visited America in the 1830s, he was struck by the middle-class character of the country and the conspicuous absence of very rich people. In Tocqueville's eyes, inured as he was to the sharp divisions between wealth and poverty in monarchical France, Americans seemed to be remarkably equal economically. Some were richer, some were poorer, but within a comparatively narrow band. Moreover, individuals had opportunities to better their economic circumstances over the course of a lifetime, and just about everybody seemed to be busy pursuing these opportunities. People who started as servants could end up as farm owners or professionals or business owners. Tocqueville believed that this combination of relative economic equality and high social mobility in some sense held the key to the American system. It was this combination of factors that defined American democracy's promise and simultaneously underwrote its stability.

President Abraham Lincoln came of age in the nineteenth-century America that Tocqueville described. Lincoln was perhaps the first American leader to fully grasp that this condition of economic opportunity was, in truth, the defining feature of America, its very essence and its justification for existing. He was the first to fully grasp the meaning of what was later called the American Dream.

The freedom guaranteed by the Declaration of Independence and the Constitution was of value, in Lincoln's view, precisely because it enabled humble individuals to attain an independent, middle-class standard of living by the work of their own hands. America was the first nation on earth to offer this opportunity of economic advancement to all, even to the humblest beginner, and this was what made the nation unique and worth preserving. Ultimately, it was the largest reason for Lincoln's willingness to fight the Civil War.

Significantly, Lincoln also believed that government had an active role to play in sustaining and underwriting this "system." If the core meaning of freedom, if the very purpose of liberty, was to enable individuals to advance economically, to improve their condition, then government's role under the Constitution must be understood in light of this principle. Government's role, in Lincoln's words, was to "clear the path" for the individual's economic advancement. In the political debates of his day, Lincoln was firmly on the side of what today we would call activist government. He favored large government expenditures for what were then called internal improvements—canals, bridges, and railroads. He believed in a strong national bank to stabilize the currency. As president, he presided over the vast federally underwritten expansion of the national railroad system and provided the first major federal funding for education with the creation of the land grant colleges. He believed, in the famous words of his Gettysburg address, that government should be not just "of the people" and "by the people," but also *for the people.*

Yet in the era of industrialization following the Civil War, a challenge arose to this vision based on a very different view of the meaning of freedom. This new view had its roots not in a political understanding of the Declaration or the Constitution, but in the laissez-faire, or "free market," thinking of British and other European economists. The new vision saw freedom not primarily as a universal promise of social mobility, but rather as an economic mechanism to produce national prosperity. Lincoln's focus was always on the fate of the ordinary worker. The new vision shifted focus to the extraordinary entrepreneur, the business owner, the industrial magnate as the engine of the new industrial prosperity. Lincoln thought government could and should enhance Americans' economic freedom by clearing the path for ordinary Americans to get ahead. The new view saw any government intervention in the economy as a severe violation of freedom and argued that government should stand aside and let business do its job. Lincoln stressed the universality of the American promise—prosperity and betterment, he repeatedly said, were to be for all. The new vision, by contrast, saw society as divided sharply between winners and losers and had little pity for the latter. Indeed, according to this new view, the very fierceness and ruthlessness of economic competition, its unbridled character, was what made prosperity grow. Under the influence of the doctrines of laissez-faire economics and Social Darwinism, the proponents of the new vision claimed that economic life—for that matter American national life—should encourage the survival of the fittest. The government should stand aside and let the laws of evolution determine who wins and who loses. Toward the end of the nineteenth century, the industrial magnate Andrew Carnegie coined a phrase that captured the essence of the new vision: "the Gospel of Wealth."[1] This new vision contemplated a society led by successful businessmen who were responsible for building a growing economy. Justice would be defined by the principle that those who contributed most to the economy deserved to be rewarded most and, in Carnegie's view, could be relied upon to use their wealth for the good of society.

In a certain sense, the two visions were easy to confuse. Both celebrated the value of economic freedom. Both sought prosperity. Both contained a rags to riches theme. But the values they represented were fundamentally at odds. Lincoln's American Dream emphasized prosperity and advancement for the ordinary worker. The Gospel of Wealth promoted worship of the exceptional individual, the millionaire, the industrial magnate, as prosperity's engine. The ideal behind the American Dream was universality and equality of opportunity. The ideal behind the Gospel of Wealth was exceptional rewards for exceptional achievement. The American Dream aspired to a middle-class society. The Gospel of Wealth was content with a society sharply divided between the rich and the poor. The

American Dream saw government as a potentially constructive force. The Gospel of Wealth saw government as a problem.

The Gospel of Wealth reigned supreme in both the Democratic and Republican administrations of the late nineteenth
century. It resurfaced in the 1920s as the dominant ideology of
the Republican Party and was embraced with fervor by Presidents Warren Harding, Calvin Coolidge, and Herbert Hoover.

Yet again and again Americans found the consequences
of the Gospel of Wealth unsustainable. Again and again, Americans insisted on a restoration of the American Dream. The major
political and economic reforms instituted under the administrations of Theodore Roosevelt, Woodrow Wilson, and Franklin Roosevelt—reforms that to a large degree built the legal
framework of the modern American economic system—can
be seen as efforts to revive the American Dream. All three presidents returned to ideals first articulated by Lincoln—Wilson
perhaps most deliberately and self-consciously, in his references
to Lincoln in campaign speeches during the election of 1912.

In his State of the Union address in 1944, President Franklin D. Roosevelt codified the essence of the Lincolnian vision
for the modern economy. He proposed "a second Bill of Rights
under which a new basis of security and prosperity can be established for all regardless of station, race or creed." He included the following among these rights:

> The right to a useful and remunerative job in the in-
> dustries or shops or farms or mines of the nation.
> The right to earn enough to provide adequate food
> and clothing and recreation.
> The right of every family to a decent home.
> The right to adequate protection from the economic
> fears of old age, sickness, accident, and unem-
> ployment.[2]

That Roosevelt's words are likely to have an odd, almost alien ring to many Americans today is a measure of how far we have come from the consensus that generally sustained American economic policy making in the decades following World War II. Today we are much less likely to speak of economic policy in such moral and political terms and much more likely to debate economic issues on technical-factual grounds that presume that the single important objective of economic policy is the growth of the economy.

It is also a sign that we live in a time when the Gospel of Wealth is again in political ascendancy.

George W. Bush echoes the rhetoric of the American Dream. But the Gospel of Wealth is clearly the basis of his policies. Nearly all the historical Gospel of Wealth themes are there: a laissez-faire economic philosophy, strong opposition to government intervention in the economy, a hatred of taxation, a desire to shrink government and strip it of resources, a celebration of the successful entrepreneur and investor as the source of prosperity and wealth—a sense that people get what they deserve out of the economy and that government has no business stepping in to even the odds. Moreover there is in the Bush program a clear rejection of Lincoln's belief that government's role is to take affirmative steps to encourage equality of opportunity.

Taxing and Spending

A major battleground of economic policy today concerns government's decisions on taxing and spending. We have made very little progress in understanding the differential economic impact of alternative tax policies—largely because political considerations tend to overwhelm factual analysis when it comes to debate about government's decisions to tax and spend.

Many politicians and economists today act as if the only relevant question is the factual one: Does the proposed policy work to increase the nation's Gross Domestic Product (GDP)? They prefer to transform economics into a purely "scientific" discipline based on mathematical analysis. They want to adopt a "value-free" perspective on the discipline of economics, where empirical questions about the impact of alternative policies on economic growth are accepted, but moral judgments about fairness and political judgments about the impact of economic policies on American democracy are excluded as "unscientific." But, in the real world of democratic politics, arguments about moral and political consequences of economic policy are unavoidable.

Americans lack clear factual answers to many of the key economic questions at issue in today's policy debate. Economic policy debates are marked by numerous unsupported assertions—which unfortunately the American public has not been in a position to evaluate on a factual basis. To take just one example: during 2001–03, President Bush and his supply-side supporters, both inside and outside his administration, presented a technical-factual argument that tax cuts—in particular, cuts in the top marginal income tax rate—would pay for themselves by increasing government tax revenues from higher economic growth.[3] But during the previous decade we had seen one of the longest sustained periods of economic growth and one of the biggest investment booms in American history, following President Clinton's *increase* in the top marginal income tax rate. Do cuts in the top marginal income tax rate increase economic growth, or don't they? Do they increase investment, or don't they? These are factual questions that should have factual answers (I'll examine the empirical evidence on these issues in chapter 8).

But factual consequences were not the only ones. President Bush's reduction of the top marginal income tax rate meant (1) a major loss of revenue for the federal treasury and (2) a sizeable tax windfall for the highest-income earners, including the multibillionaire Warren Buffetts and Bill Gateses of the world. One could argue that such a tax windfall for the highest-income citizens and their heirs was unnecessary and in some respects unfair—since such tax cuts would create deficits and could eventually lead to cuts in the necessary functions of the government. Such functions include national defense, homeland security, dealing with the consequences of natural disasters, and supporting antipoverty and pro-middle-class programs such as unemployment insurance and Social Security. Indeed, President Bush proposed such cuts in government programs at the beginning of his second term. Interestingly, Buffett, one of the country's richest men, wrote an op-ed piece for the *Washington Post* in 2003 opposing proposed cuts in taxes on dividends, arguing that he would actually end up paying a smaller percentage of his income in taxes than his office receptionist.[4] But President Bush and his economic advisers argued that tax cuts for the highest-income taxpayers, and especially cuts in the top marginal rate, were advantageous, indeed necessary, because they would increase investment, employment, and economic growth.

The president has made this argument on many occasions. To cite but one instance: "We also drop the top rate, of course, from 39.6 percent to 33 percent. If you pay taxes, you ought to get relief. Everybody who—but everybody benefits, I'm convinced, when the top rate drops because of the effect it will have on the entrepreneurial class in America. . . . And you all can help by explaining clearly to people that reducing the top rate will help with *job creation and capital formation;* and as importantly, will help highlight the American Dream" (emphasis added).[5]

The president's statement included two kinds of claims. First, cuts in the top marginal rate would increase investment (capital formation) and employment (job creation). That is a *factual* claim: that cuts in the top marginal income tax rate alter economic behavior in such a way as to cause more investment and employment (and, as a result, more economic growth). This is a claim that is either true or false; one should be able to verify it, based on data showing how the economy has performed under different tax structures. (I shall return to this question in chapter 8.) Second, the president said, "everybody benefits" because of these expected effects. This is a moral claim. Tax cuts for top-income taxpayers, the president argued, are in the interests of everybody. They serve the common good. They might not look fair at first glance, but they are fair because eventually the benefits accrue to society as a whole.

The point is that the president did not have to make this particular moral claim. He might have said alternatively that rich people ought to be able to keep the money they make, simply because they've earned it. But instead he appealed to the common good. Why? Because the president is a politician and America is a democracy. Politicians must persuade the majority that economic policies are in their interest. And in a democracy, as in any society, the rich are not the majority.

That is why issues of economic policy and issues of democratic politics are inextricably interlinked. Economic policy can go wrong in several ways. Economic policy can fail on technical grounds, simply because policymakers do not understand the impact of their policies on the workings of the economy. We have witnessed this kind of failure on a major scale twice in the past hundred years. The first episode was the Great Depression of the 1930s, and the second was the stagflation of the late 1970s, when the United States suffered from high inflation combined with high unemployment. In both cases, U.S. political leaders pursued policies that aggravated, rather than alleviated, severe economic problems. Economic policy can also fail on moral grounds, by undermining the sense of fairness on which our society depends. Such failures can lead to political instability by undermining the middle-class belief in the legitimacy of government that underpins our political democracy.

To understand all these aspects of economic policy, we must remember an ancient truth: every democracy, indeed every state, runs the risk of experiencing conflict between the few and the many. This insight originated with Aristotle. It speaks to the very nature of politics, especially democratic politics. Overcoming the potential conflict between the few and the many, the rich and the rest, has been one of the great achievements of modern American democracy—and the key to its continued stability. The basis for the solution lies in the modern industrial economy, which—unlike the agrarian economies of old—can produce *continuing* economic growth. Economic growth supported by modern technology means an ever-expanding pie. The fact that the pie is expanding means that individuals can obtain a larger piece without necessarily taking it from someone else.

Historically, the major result (and to some degree also the cause) of a growing economy has been the emergence of a strong middle class. Nearly twenty-five hundred years ago, long before the advent of modern industrialism, Aristotle observed that the most politically stable polities were democracies with a large middle class.[6] The middle class acted as a buffer between the rich, who sought to control society through their superior economic and political resources, and the many, who sought through their superior numbers to seize power from and dispossess the rich. Polities with a strong middle class were polities in which the majority had a strong stake in the continued stability of society, because such a society provided decent opportunities and a decent living for most citizens. The great consequence of the advent of modern economic life in the sixteenth and seventeenth centuries was the emergence of the middle class. America was not only the world's first democracy; it was also the first modern state to be governed, not by an aristocracy, but by a prosperous middle class.

Criteria of Judgment

The American Dream and the Gospel of Wealth propose very different specific economic policies to address the modern needs of our nation. But the specific proposals can be judged by economic, political, and moral criteria that are clear and straightforward. The economic dimension can be evaluated with the question, Does the policy increase the growth of the economy? The political dimension can be addressed with the question, Does the policy strengthen or undermine the middle class, which sustains the continued stability of our political democracy? The moral dimension of any economic policy can be addressed with the question, Is it fair to all Americans? Does it lead to an increase in inequality between the rich and the rest? or does it provide support for all members of our society?

Economic policies inevitably have large effects on the day-to-day lives of average citizens: they shape the way the costs and benefits of economic life are distributed. To put the point more directly: economic policies can create winners and losers. Contemporary arguments over tax policy start with arguments about how much revenue the government needs. But they quickly turn into arguments over how much different tax-payers should pay.

Take the income tax. Some argue for a flat tax: middle-class Americans should pay the same rate of income tax as the highest-income Americans. Others argue for a consumption tax under which middle- and lower-income families would pay taxes on a higher percentage of their income than high-income families.

For as long as the income tax has been in existence, America has preferred a progressive tax structure, by which higher-income citizens pay not only more taxes, but also a larger percentage of their income. Why? The short answer is that over time, a flat tax will create a society in which the rich get much richer than everybody else. The effect will be to create an economically polarized society. Progressive taxation is one way of softening the divide between the rich and the rest by supporting equality of opportunity for all citizens, thereby ensuring the continued strength of the middle class as democracy's center of gravity.

Average Americans are pragmatists on economic issues. The first and sometimes the only question many citizens ask about economic policy is the practical one: does it work? Economic ideology obviously plays some role in the divisions between our two major political parties. But a majority of American citizens are lost when Republican and Democratic candidates argue about the details of economic policy. They are likely to sweep either a Democratic or a Republican president from office if the results of the president's economic policies are perceived to be a practical failure. The Republican Ronald Reagan defeated the Democratic incumbent Jimmy Carter in 1980 by asking a simple question, "Are you better off now than you were four years ago?" The Democrat Bill Clinton similarly unseated the Republican president George H. W. Bush in 1992 when his campaign focused on the theme, "It's the economy, stupid!"

This pragmatism tends to go hand in hand with a "black box" attitude to economic policy. That is, most Americans are uninterested in the detailed issues and theories that swirl around the economic policy debate. Most do not focus on *how* economic policy works. They want to know *that* it works. They have little interest in looking inside the black box to see what makes it tick. As long as the black box yields good results, they are satisfied. Only if they see economic failure—as reflected in a downturn of their economic fortunes and those of their neighbors—are they inclined to ask deeper policy questions.

That is why, at the end of the day, opinion polling on specific economic issues such as taxes, spending, deficits, Social Security, Medicaid, and other federal programs cumulatively yield an ambiguous picture. Using different selective sets of polling numbers, one could easily make the case that, on economic issues, the American people are dominantly conservative or liberal, right-leaning or left-leaning. In reality, many Americans have ambivalent positions on the theoretical side of these questions. The situation is reminiscent of the story told about the congressional candidate in Texas who went to a small town and gave an earnest speech about the problems of ignorance and apathy. Afterward, he went to the town tavern and asked one of the men sitting at the bar what he thought of the speech. The man turned to him and said, "I don't know, and I don't care."

In one way, this general lack of interest in the details of economic policy can be a plus: it saves us from the paralysis of severe political polarization along class lines. The politics of economic class has generally played a lesser role in the United States than in the nations of Western Europe—and all to the good. In another way, though, Americans' lack of interest in the specifics of economic policy creates problems. It prevents citizens from connecting the dots in ways that would help them protect their interests. For example, few voters entering the polls in November 2004 understood that President Bush's 2001–03 tax cuts, by wiping out federal surpluses and creating large federal deficits, had in effect made the coming Social Security crisis less manageable. President Bush took up the Social Security issue only after the election in January 2005. At that time, he argued that there was an urgent Social Security financial crisis on the horizon that must be dealt with. Whatever Social Security crisis there was, Bush's first-term tax cuts had made it very much worse: they had eliminated federal funds that could have been used to meet Social Security's obligations relatively painlessly for years to come. What few middle-class voters understood was that the few hundred dollars they saved in income taxes in those years would likely be taken back from them or their children later—in the form of increased Social Security taxes, reduced Social Security benefits, or a reduction in the financial capability of the federal government to pay for other essentials such as unemployment insurance, national defense, homeland security, or relief following natural disasters such as Hurricanes Katrina and Rita.

The lack of information about the specific consequences of individual economic policies opens the door to widespread demagoguery on these issues. Economic policy debate in the United States can be likened to a big snake oil yard sale, where what are offered are half-truths, myths, and canards. A major task we confront as citizens is to cut through the economic myth-making and get at the truth. There is no greater antidote to myth than history. To understand where we are headed economically, it is vital to understand where we have been. The first American statesman to fully comprehend the meaning of the American economic vision was Abraham Lincoln.

Chapter II
Lincoln's Economics: The Origins of the American Dream

This middle-class country had got
a middle-class president, at last.
—*Eulogy to Abraham Lincoln by Ralph Waldo Emerson*

Abraham Lincoln was not only a moral leader; he was also a political philosopher and an economic realist. We so fully undersatnd Abraham Lincoln's contribution to our nation's *moral* beliefs that we have neglected his role in shaping our uniquely American *economic* vision. Because the moral issues surrounding the slavery question are so clear to us today, there is a tendency to understand the origins of the American Civil War solely in this familiar moral context. In actuality, the Civil War was fought not just about slavery, but about what kind of economy the nation would have. It was a moral clash, and it was also a clash between two economic systems.

Lincoln's genius lay in his ability to discern the relationship between the workaday, economic realities of American life and the nation's highest moral and political principles. In Lincoln's mind, the opportunity "to improve one's condition" was an essential feature of the Declaration of Independence's claim that human beings have unalienable rights to "life, liberty, and the pursuit of happiness." To Lincoln, the economic, moral, and political elements were inextricably intertwined. Together, they represented what is distinctively American about our economy and democracy. "I have never had a feeling politically," Lincoln said, "that did not spring from the sentiments embodied in the Declaration of Independence."[1] The reason that "government of the people, by the people, and for the people" was worth preserving—and even worth fighting a war to preserve—was precisely that it offered this opportunity to each American "to improve one's condition."

More than any other president, Lincoln is the father of the American Dream that all Americans should have the opportunity through hard work to build a comfortable middle-class life. For Lincoln, liberty meant above all the right of individuals to the fruits of their own labor, seen as a path to prosperity. "To [secure] to each labourer the whole product of his labour, or as nearly as possible," he wrote, "is a most worthy object of any good government." The real evil of the southern slave system was the denial of this economic right. Indeed, Lincoln insisted that African Americans were entitled to the same *economic* rights as all other Americans, even putting these ahead of such political rights as full citizenship or voting rights.

The purpose of the United States was to "clear the path" for the individual to labor and get ahead. Lincoln understood that this purpose was challenged by the slave-based, aristocratic economic system of the southern states. It was this challenge that created a house divided: virtually two separate nations based on very different economic structures. He saw "saving the Union" not simply as a political effort but as a moral imperative to secure for the America of the future the middle-class economy of the northern states.

For Lincoln, American liberty was intimately connected with economic opportunity. It was economic opportunity that gave liberty meaning. The universal promise of opportunity was for Lincoln the philosophical core of America; it was the essence of the American system. "Without the *Constitution* and the *Union*," he wrote, "we could not have attained . . . our great prosperity." But the Constitution and the Union were not the "primary cause" of America, Lincoln believed. "There is something," he continued, "back of these, entwining itself more closely about the human heart. That something, is the principle of 'Liberty to all'—the principle that clears the *path* for all—gives *hope* to all—and, by consequence, *enterprise,* and *industry* to all." "The prudent, penniless beginner in the world," Lincoln wrote, "labors for wages awhile, saves a surplus with which to buy tools or land for himself, then labors on his own account another while, and at length hires another new beginner to help him. This is the just and generous and prosperous system which opens the way to all, gives hope to all, and consequent energy and progress and improvement of condition to all."[2] This was, for Lincoln, the American Dream, the raison d'être of America, and the unique contribution of America to world history.

President Abraham Lincoln was the first American leader to fully grasp that this condition of economic opportunity was, in truth, the defining feature of America, its very essence and its justification for existing. He was the first to fully grasp the meaning of what was later called the American Dream.

The freedom guaranteed by the Declaration of Independence and the Constitution was of value, in Lincoln's view, precisely because it enabled humble individuals to attain an independent, middle-class standard of living by the work of their own hands. America was the first nation on earth to offer this opportunity of economic advancement to all, even to the humblest beginner, and this was what made the nation unique and worth preserving. Ultimately, it was the largest reason for Lincoln's willingness to fight the Civil War.

As he noted in a message to Congress in March 1861, at the outset of the Civil War, "On the side of the Union is a struggle for maintaining in the world that form and substance of government whose *leading object* is to elevate the condition of men to lift artificial weights from all shoulders; to clear the paths of laudable pursuit for all; to afford all an unfettered start, and a *fair chance in the race of life*" (emphasis added).[3] Or as he said while campaigning for president in 1860, "I want every man to have the chance—and I believe a black man is entitled to it—in which he can better his condition—when he may look forward and hope to be a hired laborer this year and the next, work for himself afterward, and finally to hire men to work for him! That is the true system."[4]

Throughout his political life, Lincoln supported policies that would sustain and expand this "system." He was on one side of major partisan political struggles over tariffs, "internal improvements," a national bank, and ultimately the issue of the expansion of slavery in the territories. These struggles culminated in an all-out confrontation between North and South over two alternative ways of life. But whether the issue was tariffs, internal improvements, a sound currency, or the expansion of a southern economy based on slavery, Lincoln's fealty was always to the system. In the final analysis, Lincoln did not fight the Civil War to end slavery, though that was the war's great result. Lincoln fought the Civil War to vindicate and preserve the American Dream.

The Origin of the Dream

A well-known encyclopedia of words and phrases incorrectly attributes the phrase "American Dream" to the nineteenth-century French writer Alexis de Tocqueville.[5] In reality, the phrase was first popularized a century later by the historian James Truslow Adams, in a best-selling book, *The Epic of America* (1932).[6] But the encyclopedia error is fruitful, for Tocqueville's book *Democracy in America,* based on his travels in the United States in the early 1830s, provides us with the first real glimpse of what the American Dream was about. Tocqueville described the very world in which Lincoln labored, advanced, and succeeded. The Frenchman's American journey concluded in 1832, the very year in which Lincoln entered politics as a candidate for the Illinois State Assembly. Viewing this early American economy through Tocqueville's eyes is a way to understand the unique opportunity Lincoln saw.

"Amongst the novel objects that attracted my attention during my stay in the United States," Tocqueville began his account, "nothing struck me more forcibly than the general equality of conditions."[7] Tocqueville witnessed a land alive with individual enterprise, a land in which virtually all citizens, some a bit poorer, some a bit richer, but very few "very rich" by European standards, strove tirelessly to better their condition and in the process transformed the American landscape.[8]

Of course, the country was tailor-made for those seeking to improve their fortunes, with its virtually limitless land, a wealth of natural resources, and a geographical location that guaranteed the security necessary for the flourishing of commerce by providing the barrier of an ocean against Europe's conflicts and wars.[9]

Tocqueville was struck by the level of social mobility.[10] Not only were the differences in wealth between rich and poor much narrower than in Europe, but also most of the wealthy persons he met had made rather than inherited their fortunes. Even the poor expected to be wealthy some day. "I never met in America," he noted, "with any citizen so poor as not to cast a glance of hope and envy on the enjoyments of the rich, or whose imagination did not possess itself by anticipation of those good things which fate still obstinately withheld from him."[11]

The fact that most Americans were neither rich nor poor—the middle-class nature of the nation—lent American society enormous stability, in Tocqueville's view. In combination with the opportunities for social mobility, the nation's middle-class nature was a barrier to social upheaval and revolution: "Between these two extremes of [wealth and poverty in] democratic communities stand an innumerable multitude of men almost alike, who, without being exactly either rich or poor, are possessed of sufficient property to desire the maintenance of order, yet not enough to excite envy. Such men are the natural enemies of violent commotions; their lack of agitation keeps all beneath them and above them still, and secures the balance of the fabric of society."[12]

A Nation in Search of Its Soul

America, seen through Tocqueville's eyes, was clearly some-thing new and different. But for much of the first "fourscore and seven years" of its existence, America was still a nation in search of an identity. Some of the most fundamental questions concerning what America was about remained unanswered and indeed were only beginning to be asked.

Perhaps the most fundamental question of all was the meaning of the Union itself. Only with great difficulty had the Framers of the Constitution yoked the thirteen separate for-mer colonies into a United States. Today time and long usage have led us to think of our fifty states as something akin to provinces, administrative and geographic units of a larger, uni-fied nation. Only perhaps at our quadrennial political conven-tions, when the "great state of Ohio" or the "great state of Illi-nois" casts its votes for presidential nominees, are we reminded of the once independent character of these entities. When Americans before Lincoln's era heard the word "state," they heard a strong echo of the word as it is used today in the field of international relations—the way in which we say that France, Germany, and the United Kingdom are states. "United States" was not yet a singular, but a plural noun. Politicians routinely spoke of "these United States," meaning independent, sover-eign states unified under an agreed-on federal government. But whether this federal government was a strong federation or a loose confederacy remained in dispute. Many important politicians found themselves on different sides of that question, depending on the issue at stake. Even such figures as the Kentuckian Henry Clay, perhaps the nation's leading proponent of a stronger and more active federal government during Lincoln's first decades in politics, still had a strong sense of states' rights.

In one sense the political issues that dominated Lincoln's age were quite different from those of our era. In another sense, they were somewhat the same. Many of the debates of the 1830s and 1840s were about whether there should be more or less government—meaning the federal government. Perhaps surprisingly, Lincoln—despite or rather because of his ardent belief in individual economic opportunity—was firmly on the side of those who favored more.

"My politics are short and sweet, like the old woman's dance," Lincoln told audiences when he ran for a seat in the Illinois State Assembly in 1832. "I am in favor of a national bank. I am in favor of the internal improvement system and a high protective tariff."[13] Lincoln's quip summarized the three key issues that divided the nation, and the political parties, in the decades leading up to the Civil War, before the issue of slavery overwhelmed them all: the national bank, tariffs, and government expenditures for internal improvements.

Lincoln entered politics as a Whig, in particular as a follower of Henry Clay. Clay, senator, congressman, secretary of state, Speaker of the House, was a national politician who ran unsuccessfully for president five times. He was the nation's leading proponent of a strong Union and a strengthened federal government. By the mid-1820s, he had devised a political program under the nicely saleable label of the American System (when Lincoln, as he often did, used the word "system" in politics, he was consciously echoing Clay). Clay's American System program had three components: a national bank, to provide the nation with a sound currency and stable financial system; high tariffs, to encourage the growth of domestic manufacturing; and federal spending, financed by tariffs, to create roads, bridges, canals, and other transportation infrastructure to aid in the development of the domestic economy.[14] Lincoln's "old woman's dance" was an echo of Clay's program.

A Bottom-Up Vision

Clay and his Whig party were the political heirs of Alexander Hamilton and the Federalists. Clay, like Hamilton, was primarily nationalistic in his motivation. He was concerned about the relative strength of the United States as a world power. In 1812, he had been a leader of the War Hawks, who agitated for war with Great Britain. When that ill-advised conflict resulted disastrously in the British sack of the nation's capital and the burning of the White House, Clay became even more convinced of the need for a strengthened central government, with renewed military power, an infrastructure of good roads (for both economic and military purposes), and a large, independent manufacturing sector that would insulate the nation from dependence on Britain for manufactured goods. Clay also saw his American System as something that would aid the common people—by promoting economic development. He always claimed to have a concern for ordinary citizens. And he certainly believed in America as a land of opportunity and saw his American System as a way to expand opportunities. Clay was responsible for putting the term "self-made man" into political circulation. But in truth, his concern with the welfare of workers was generally secondary to his nationalistic ambitions for the United States, his vision of America as an emerging world power.[15]

Lincoln's vision came from his personal experiences. His perspective was that of a man starting humbly who had worked his way up the social and economic ladder by sheer discipline, persistence, and force of will; it was a perspective he never lost. It shaped his core values. "I hold the value of life is to improve one's condition," he told an audience in Cincinnati in 1861. "Whatever is calculated to advance the condition of the honest, struggling laboring man, I am for that thing." Or as he sympathetically told a delegation of striking workers who visited the White House in 1863, "I know the trials and woes of workingmen. I have always felt for them."[16]

When Lincoln embraced Clay's economic system, he did so not out of a sense of nationalism but because in very practical terms, he thought Clay's program would aid ordinary working people, people like himself, those striving to become, and remain, middle class. As an inhabitant of a still-undeveloped frontier state, an Illinois bereft of decent roads and dependably navigable rivers—to say nothing of canals and railroads—he saw a need for government to act, to provide the infrastructure that would allow the expansion of internal commerce, to guarantee a sound currency to enable economic transactions, and to protect homegrown manufacturing from the threat of (mostly British) manufactured goods from abroad. The government's job was to "clear the path" for its citizens to get ahead. The whole nation had witnessed the vast benefits that accrued to the citizens of New York from the construction of the Erie Canal. Lincoln wanted something of the same for his own citizens of Illinois. While Clay sought, with limited success, to promote internal improvements at the federal level, Lincoln pursued a similar program at the level of state government.

At bottom, there was a philosophical logic to Lincoln's

Whigism. The founding principle of the nation was liberty. The purpose of liberty was to enable individuals to improve their condition. The role of government therefore was to serve that central purpose by, as Lincoln liked to put it, "clearing the path" for men to achieve economic success. "Clearing the path" for Lincoln meant more than government getting out of the way. Clearing the path was a frontier metaphor, suggestive of the hard work of clearing forest for a farm or a road, pulling stumps and rocks out of the ground with teams of oxen. "The legitimate object of government," he wrote in a note around 1854, "is 'to do for the people what needs to be done, but which they can not, by individual effort, do at all, or do so well, for themselves.'" Like political philosophers from the time of Thomas Hobbes and John Locke, Lincoln saw the first purpose of government as providing for physical security and the common defense. But he also believed that government should take positive action to promote the common good: "There are many such things—some of them exist independently of the injustice of the world. Making and maintaining roads, bridges, and the like; providing for the helpless young and afflicted; common schools; and disposing of deceased men's property are instances." He saw "charities, pauperism, orphanage" as government responsibilities.[17] Not that Lincoln believed government's role should be intrusive; he thought it should be limited. But by the standards of his time, when the federal government was minimal and even state governments often had few resources at their disposal, he was in favor of activist government—on the grounds that the whole purpose of the United States was to serve the individual's economic opportunity and that government should play its proper role in assisting this effort. His major undertaking when he entered the Illinois State Assembly was to push through an ambitious package of internal improvements, partially state-financed roads, bridges, canals, and railroads.

The Jacksonians

If the drive for economic advancement and material progress represented one great thrust of our early national life, then the other great thrust was toward increasing political democracy. In the years leading up to Lincoln's entry into politics, most states had expanded their suffrage to include not just property owners but all free white males. The expansion of voting rights in the decades since the Founding had given a new, more raucous, more populist cast to national politics. No one better epitomized this new populism than President Andrew Jackson. On the occasion of his inauguration in 1829, he famously opened the doors of the White House to one and all. Farmers stood on the fine chairs in their muddy boots. Damage to the presidential residence by the end of the affair was in the thousands of dollars. But the point had been made. The people were now in charge.

Jackson, "Old Hickory," the wrathful general, the hero of New Orleans and many other battles, was also Clay's archrival and nemesis. Like Clay he was for Union and Liberty, but he understood them in very different terms.

As Clay's politics looked back to Hamilton, so Jackson's looked back to Jefferson. Clay's—and Lincoln's—mind was on manufacturing (Lincoln despised farming, partly because of memories of his own miserable experiences working his father's land, partly from his conclusion that farming offered no quick path to economic success). Jackson was a North Carolina plantation owner. His mentality was agrarian, at a time when the vast majority of Americans, landowners and labor-

ers alike, were still engaged in agriculture. Where Clay and
Lincoln saw an active federal government as a tool to expand
opportunity, Jackson, like Jefferson before him, strove to preserve the Union but saw a strong central government as a potential threat to liberty.

Many historians have seen in Jackson a kind of founding
father of the modern Democratic Party. But on economic policy the positions of Jackson's Democratic Party bore a closer
resemblance to those of today's Republicans than to those of
today's Democrats. The Jacksonian Democratic Party was, in
present-day terms, anti–big government, viewing with deep
suspicion economic development, urbanization, and virtually
all the other developments the Whigs saw as progress. Jackson's economic policy approach was of a piece with his skepticism about what we would call today the public sector.

Two Economic Systems

Jackson's attack on the activist American System proposed by
Clay was manifested in his destruction of the Second Bank of
the United States. Jackson's suspicion of the bank carried with
it an element of sectionalism. He thought the bank disproportionately benefited northern financial interests. The bank had
had its share of problems, but on the whole it lent a vital stability to the nation's financial system. Jackson's destruction of
the bank would condemn the nation to currency instability
and a terrible cycle of booms and busts for decades to come.
Jackson also demonstrated his opposition to internal improvements by vetoing bills to provide federal aid for the construction of roads.

The most explosive issue facing American politicians
North and South proved to be the tariff. Tariffs were the finan-

cial centerpiece of Clay's American System. As Speaker of the House, he had engineered passage of a major tariff bill in 1824—the first true protective tariff in American history. From the start, much of the South opposed tariffs because their main purpose was to protect domestic manufacturing, largely a northern enterprise. At the same time, in the southern view, tariffs threatened the southern economy, which was critically dependent on trade with Great Britain. Great Britain was by far the United States' largest trading partner in the antebellum era, and the most important American export to Britain was southern cotton.

It should come as no surprise that the South opposed not only high tariffs but also federal government expenditures for internal improvements. Southern politicians questioned the constitutionality of such ambitious federal action. They argued that these activist government programs unduly benefited northern financial and industrial interests. In the South the idea of public investment in infrastructure remained largely an alien notion. Southern legislatures were controlled by slaveholders, who had little economic interest in public improvements, no need to create an active economy for a free labor force, and a substantial ability to surround themselves with luxury in the private preserve of their plantations. The southern political mind increasingly viewed both tariffs and internal improvements as northern ideas.

In the decades before the Civil War, the notion of material progress and the dream of social mobility took fire in the northern mind. Northern and western states from New York to Illinois actively pursued internal improvements and built up their public infrastructure to support this dream. By contrast, pursuing social mobility through social improvements offered no positive benefit, in the southern view.

America was increasingly dividing into two distinct sectional societies. The North was expanding its internal industrial capacity, while the South remained anchored in a highly profitable slave-based agricultural economy, heavily reliant on cotton exports to Great Britain.

Two different economies, with divergent and in many respects opposed sets of interests coexisted under one flag. And with the two economies came two cultures and worldviews, North and South. More and more, economic policy disputes were coming to be seen through the sectional lens. The growing sectional divide—the growing crisis between North and South—*initially played out as a struggle over economic policy, and only later as an explicit conflict over slavery.*

The House Divided

The economic battles over tariffs, internal improvements, and the national bank were important in their own right. But they were also surrogates for an emerging moral struggle that would explode in the mid-1850s. In the North the abolitionist movement was growing. Abolitionists flooded Congress with petitions against slavery. In the mid-1830s, Congress began passing annual "gag rules" to prevent discussion of the issue in the House and Senate. Northern Democrats like Stephen Douglas hated the abolitionist campaign, not as partisans of slavery, but, in their view, as statesmen dedicated to the preservation of the Union. They saw the more extreme manifestations of both northern and southern sectionalism as a dire threat to the Union.

During the three decades before the Civil War, politicians dedicated to the Union, on both sides of the slavery question, struggled to keep the division over slavery from tearing the nation apart. What ultimately forced the issue was the nation's continued westward expansion. Would the new states added to the Union have an economy based on slave labor or free labor? The repeal of the Missouri Compromise with the passage of Douglas's Kansas–Nebraska Act in 1854, which allowed Kansas and Nebraska to choose by popular sovereignty, forced the issue of slavery to the center of the national stage. It brought the long-seething conflict to the heart of national life.

In 1858, in a speech at the Republican State Convention in Springfield, Lincoln threw down the gauntlet to the slave states:

> Under the operation of the policy of compromise, the slavery agitation has not only not ceased, but has constantly augmented. In my opinion it will not cease until a crisis shall have been reached and passed. "A house divided against itself cannot stand." I believe this government cannot endure permanently half slave and half free. I do not expect the Union to be dissolved. I do not expect the house to fall, but I do expect it will cease to be divided. It will become all one thing or all the other; either the opponents of slavery will arrest the further spread of it, and place it where the public mind shall rest in the belief that it is in the course of ultimate extinction, or its advocates will push it forward till it shall become alike lawful in all the States, old as well as new, North as well as South.[18]

Because the moral issues surrounding the slavery debate are so clear to us today there is a tendency to understand the origins of the American Civil War solely in its moral context.

More than is often realized, the Civil War was fought not about the morality of slavery, but about what kind of economy the nation would have. It was a moral clash, but it was also a clash between two economic systems. It is difficult to grasp the degree to which the United States, on the eve of the Civil War, had truly evolved into a "house divided," virtually two separate nations based on very different economic structures.

What the North feared most was the spread of the southern economic culture. The question was which economy would define the future of America as it migrated westward, that of the North or of the South? The fear, shared by Lincoln, was that the American dream would no longer sustain American society, that slave labor would ultimately drive out free labor, first in the West and then later perhaps in the country as a whole.

By 1854, Whigs and antislavery former Democrats had combined to form the new Republican Party. What ultimately unified the Republican Party was an *economic vision*—quite different in important respects from that of the Republican Party later in the nineteenth century and that of the Republican Party today. Lincoln was the best and most philosophical, though by no means the only, exponent of this new outlook. Its watchword was the concept of free labor. We have already seen the vision in outline. But now it becomes especially clear against the background of its alternative—which was the aristocratic economic life as it was known in the slave-owning South. The vision, especially in Lincoln's hands, was aimed primarily at improving the lot of ordinary citizens, of creating and sustaining a middle-class country.

When his hero Henry Clay died in 1852, Lincoln delivered a eulogy in Springfield, parts of which were less a description of Clay than a thinly veiled self-portrait. The heart of the eulogy is a description of the very philosophical core of Lincoln's

political and economic philosophy, which he artfully attributed to Clay: "Mr. Clay's predominant sentiment, from first to
last, was a deep devotion to the cause of human liberty—a strong
sympathy with the oppressed everywhere, and an ardent wish
for their elevation. With him this was a primary and all-
controlling passion. . . . He desired the prosperity of his countrymen, partly because they were his countrymen, but chiefly to
show to the world that free men could be prosperous."[19]

For Lincoln, liberty meant above all the right of individuals to the fruits of their own labor, seen as a path to prosperity: "To [secure] to each labourer the whole product of his
labour, or as nearly as possible," he wrote, "is a most worthy
object of any good government." The real evil of slavery, in
Lincoln's view, was precisely the denial of this right. Interestingly, in his campaign for president, Lincoln emphasized the
rights of African Americans to the same *economic rights* as all
other Americans, setting these economic rights ahead of such
issues as full citizenship or voting rights. The whole purpose of
the United States was to clear the path for the individual to
labor and get ahead. The emphasis was always on government's duty to the whole people and especially to ordinary, un-
privileged people.[20]

Significantly, for Lincoln and the new Republican Party
the doctrine of free labor implied an *active role for government*
in fulfilling this mission. It was the slave-owning South, rather
than the Republican North, which adhered to the doctrine of
pure free market economics. It was the slave-owning South
that sought to diminish the size and powers of the federal government. It was the slave owners of the South, secure in their
vast personal wealth, who saw little point to investments in the
public sector to build a national infrastructure. It was the South

that was sharply divided between the few rich and the many poor: a region with minimal social mobility and no ethic of social responsibility.

It was this active role of government that Lincoln alluded to in the now most famous phrase from his Gettysburg Address. The essence of the United States was not merely government "of the people" and "by the people," but also government "for the people," government in an active role clearing the path for its citizens to advance economically.

Clay never saw his American System come to full fruition. But, as president, Lincoln was able to implement many of Clay's ideas and a few more of his own. Lincoln, notes the historian Gabor Boritt, "had the pleasure of signing into law much of the program he had worked for through the better part of his political career." As president, Lincoln presided over measures that decisively strengthened the role of the government in American economic life. In the process he created what Leonard P. Curry has called "a blueprint for modern America."[21]

Lincoln signed into law the National Banking Act, which not only revived the national bank, but gave the country its first unified currency (until then states and state banks had created their own money) and created a system of chartered national banks throughout the states. The Homestead Act provided land inexpensively to settlers willing to migrate west. Lincoln raised tariffs to encourage the development of domestic manufacturing. He chartered the first transcontinental railroad, which would link the country from East to West Coasts, the greatest internal improvement up to that time. He signed the Morrill Act, which granted land to states to establish colleges, the beginnings of the nation's state university system—designed to clear the path for ordinary people to secure an education and achieve the American economic dream. All were embodiments of what Lincoln believed to be government's legitimate and vital role.

The economic challenges facing Lincoln are in some respects very different from the issues that perplex us today. But Lincoln, as our most clear-eyed president, was the first to fully understand what America is all about and to tell us so in unfailingly clear terms. He lived in a "house divided" between two ways of life. On the one side was a middle-class society honoring labor and offering multiple opportunities for economic advancement by ordinary people, where government was assuming an increasingly constructive role in clearing the path for economic success. On the other side was a society rigidly divided between rich and poor, ensuring through law and oppression that labor remained devalued and cheap, dedicated to an unfettered free market, neglectful of the public sector and offering few if any opportunities for ordinary people, and none at all for a whole race of human beings. For Lincoln, the choice was never a hard one. He consecrated his life to ensuring that "government of the people, by the people, and for the people, shall not perish from the face of the earth." In doing so, he showed us the principled criteria by which American economic policy needs to be judged. Today, in evaluating our economic policies, it is useful to ask Lincoln's questions again. Is our nation's economic policy in the service of the middle-class ideal, the dream of America—to enable ordinary people to get ahead? Is our government truly "for the people"?

Chapter III
The Gospel of Wealth

The decades following the Civil War were a period of unprecedented industrial growth and economic and social transformation in the United States. Literally within the span of a generation, America grew from a dominantly agrarian nation into the world's leading industrial power. The transformation of the American landscape was epochal. From 1870 to 1900, railroad mileage more than tripled, while steel production increased by more than a hundredfold. In the same period, overall manufacturing output quadrupled, while agriculture's share of the economy declined. An abundance of new products became available, and a national system of commerce emerged, linking farmers and manufacturers alike to markets North, South, East, and West. Overall, between 1870 and 1900, U.S. Gross National Product more than tripled in real terms, with manufacturing accounting for an ever-increasing share of output.[1]

Economic life also began to be organized in larger and larger units. Between 1850 and 1880, the corporation became the standard business entity. And many corporations were in

turn absorbed into larger "trusts," as ambitious industrial magnates sought to achieve monopoly power over specific markets. John D. Rockefeller organized the Standard Oil Trust,
which by 1879 controlled 90 percent of the nation's refining industry. By 1904, there were over three hundred such powerful
industrial combinations holding dominant positions in a vari-
ety of industries.[2]

Even before the Civil War, the old system of independent
artisans and home-based manufacturing was in decline; production was increasingly shifting to large mills and factories,
driven by water and steam power. There, scores and sometimes
hundreds of workers labored long hours in harsh conditions,
churning out a growing flood of textiles, shoes, and other consumer and durable goods. A major source of labor for the
growing industries was the swelling millions of immigrants—
some 13.5 million between 1865 and 1900—who poured into
tenement neighborhoods in New York and other cities of the
North.[3] With the immigrants came the predictable manifestations of poverty and social disorder.

Enormous amounts of money were being made, but it
was increasingly concentrated in very few hands. By 1890, the
richest 1 percent of the population was absorbing half of the
entire national income and controlled more than half the nation's wealth.[4]

As industrial life came to be organized on a larger scale,
the size of the federal government also significantly expanded.
In 1860, on the eve of the Civil War, federal outlays totaled just
over $63 million. By 1865, the war's last year, outlays had risen
to $1.3 billion. Demobilization following the war led to a sharp
cutback in federal expenditures. But even in 1870, the federal
government was still spending some $310 million a year, five
times what it had spent a decade earlier.[5] Many of these mil-

lions were finding their way, via government loans and other subsidies, into the hands of railroad magnates and other businessmen who secured special favors from the federal government. Lincoln and the Republicans had won the argument in favor of internal improvements, and certainly the construction of the railroads—financed by millions in free government land grants and millions more in generous federal loans—supported the country's economic development. But the prediction of some opponents of such substantial government expenditures was also borne out: the new millions in government funds formed a seemingly irresistible temptation to corruption. President Ulysses S. Grant's two terms from 1869 through 1876 were marred by an endless string of major scandals, in which executive branch officials and various members of Congress were exposed as colluding with industrialists to enrich themselves at taxpayer expense.

Corruption at the federal level was mirrored in the big cities, where political machines seized power and, by trading jobs and favors for votes, maintained control of city hall and siphoned off thousands, sometimes millions, in graft, patronage, and kickbacks. The bright side of the machines is that they provided a kind of unofficial support network for newly arriving immigrants. The dark side is that they stole the public treasury blind. William M. "Boss" Tweed's notorious Tammany Hall machine managed to bilk perhaps as much as $100 million out of New York City taxpayers before it was finally overthrown.[6]

American politics in the years before and during the Civil War had been marked by high idealism—elevated debates about the meaning of democracy, the nature of labor, and the future of the nation. By the end of the war, with over six hundred thousand dead on the two sides, Americans were understandably exhausted at the prospect of further ideological struggle. In the end Republican and Democratic policies were often indistinguishable. James Bryce, an English aristocrat who wrote a book about his own Tocqueville-like tour of the United States in the late 1880s, noted that "neither party has any principles, any distinctive tenets." "All has been lost," he wrote, "except office or the hope of it."[7] Both parties claimed to champion the interests of the common citizen, but neither party had a program for doing so.

It was a time when those who could do so grabbed for the "fast buck," and when those who could not generally settled for their meager lot in life. It was an era when money talked more loudly than ideas. In an 1876 novel, Mark Twain and Charles Dudley Warner dubbed it the Gilded Age.[8]

The Transformation of Free Labor

No one can say whether President Lincoln, had he survived to complete his second term, would have been able to translate his vision of the American Dream into a coherent peacetime economic program. The struggle over slavery, and the war itself, eclipsed concerns about economics, even as the economy was beginning to undergo rapid change to a new society dominated by large manufacturing concerns and industrial wage earners.

At all events, the disappearance of Lincoln opened the way for the transformation of Lincoln's free labor idea into something gradually resembling its opposite. The agents of this transformation were a new generation of intellectuals—in a sense, America's first crop of urban intellectuals—variously called liberals, radicals, and, in perhaps the most entertaining political moniker in American history, mugwumps. (The last label, from an Algonquin word meaning "big chief," was slapped on the reformers by the *New York Sun* when many of them bolted the Republican Party in 1884 to campaign for the Democrat Grover Cleveland. The implication was that they believed themselves too good for the Republican Party and its candidate, James G. Blaine.)[9]

The mugwumps were a mixed group. Many, like the German-born politician Carl Schurz, had strong roots in the prewar Republican Party; generally abolitionist in sentiment, they had been free labor, free soil men before the war. But, there was also new blood. The journalist E. L. Godkin, born in Northern Ireland, educated at Queen's College, Belfast, and in London, arrived in the United States in the 1850s brimming with the new ideas of the British political economists. In 1865, with the help of the Harvard-educated writer-scholar Charles Eliot Norton and the Philadelphia abolitionist James Miller McKim, he founded the journal the *Nation,* which became a kind of flagship publication for what they called reform. Others, such as Charles Francis Adams and Henry Adams, were scions of old American families. By and large, the backbone of the mugwump movement was a rentier class, perhaps the first representatives of such a class to exist in America, the college-educated, leisured young heirs of the old merchant, manufacturing, and banking families of the Northeast (along with some sons of well-heeled clergymen and professors). Godkin at one point referred to this social group as the "unemployed rich."[10]

They styled themselves the champions of reform. But in retrospect their program seemed strangely disconnected from the real problems of their age, in particular, the growing plight of the industrial worker. To be sure, at the core of their vision was an understandable revulsion from the corruption that had come to dominate Gilded Age politics. They felt that instead of the collection of scoundrels populating Grant's administration or the crude, uncultured machine bosses that ruled the cities, it was they and men like them who should rightly govern. Government should be run by the "best men," and in their own minds they fit that description. They were educated, cultured, wise, and incorruptible, and they had the public interest at heart. Besides, they were also in possession of what they considered the modern scientific understanding of the eternal laws of political economy, which in their view held the key to wise governance.[11]

Lincoln's American Dream was essentially homegrown: it emerged from his understanding of the connection between the principles embodied in the Declaration and his firsthand experience of the opportunities of American economic life. The new economic vision of the reformers was a foreign import, largely from Great Britain. Its source was the new "science" of "political economy," what today we would call free market economics. From Adam Smith to David Ricardo and John Stuart Mill, two generations of British thinkers had sought to place the study of economics on a systematic, scientific footing.

Especially as it was understood by this new generation of American intellectuals, the new economic science had as its central tenet the nonintervention of government in economic life. At the time, the term of art for nonintervention was the French phrase "laissez-faire," meaning, essentially, "leave it be" or "leave it alone."

Under the influence of the new economic doctrine, the notion of free labor came to be understood in terms quite different from those embraced by Lincoln. It meant, essentially, that the laborer was on his own. Even as modern factories multiplied, destroying the old artisan system of manufacturing and driving millions of workers into increasingly desperate circumstances, with long hours, dangerous and unhealthy working conditions, and pay below subsistence levels, the self-styled reformers adamantly resisted government intervention. They opposed legislation on the eight-hour day and disparaged proposals for child labor laws. They wrote diatribes against unions and labor leaders.

Soon the new economics blended with an even harsher social doctrine based on extrapolations of Charles Darwin's new theory of evolution to human economics. Social Darwinism saw human economic life as analogous to the process of evolution: economic outcomes reflected the "survival of the fittest"—a phrase coined by the English thinker Herbert Spencer, whose books proved massively popular among the American reformers.[12] Those who prospered economically were the fit; those who labored long hours in factories for below subsistence wages were demonstrably the unfit. The growing inequality that America witnessed between a tiny group of superrich industrialists and a mass of increasingly degraded and impoverished workers was actually seen as a sign of social progress; it was good for maximum economic growth and the advancement of the race, a necessary price of progress toward ever-greater national wealth and prosperity. Social Darwinism integrated the ideas of laissez-faire economics and evolution into a new doctrine that not only forbad government intervention in the economy, but also provided a moral justification for harsh working conditions and growing economic inequality.

The mugwumps looked askance both at those who stood above them and those who stood below them on the economic ladder. They saw themselves as being caught between "an ignorant proletariat and half-taught plutocracy," in the words of the historian Francis Parkman. On the one hand, they despised the rapacious Robber Barons (it was Godkin who coined the term in 1867 to describe the crude, allegedly self-made railroad magnates who absorbed millions in government loans and then exerted monopoly-like control over the communities that grew up along their rail lines). On the other hand, they disparaged the unwashed masses of workers—the "ignorant proletariat"— who threatened domestic tranquility with growing labor agitation. These they regarded as the "dangerous classes." While the reformers professed equal dislike for the monopoly trusts and organized labor, "they seemed far more alarmed by [the] growing political danger from below," as the historian John Sproat has written.[13]

At one level, the mugwumps' peculiarly reactionary response to the plight of labor was simply a failure to understand the new industrial realities. It was as though they retained in their minds the image of the independent free labor craftsmen who dominated the pre–Civil War American economy. They saw the laborer as freely negotiating the sale of his labor, as if he were an independent agent, unhampered by the hard new economic realities of a factory-based economy. "The right of each man to labor as much or as little as he chooses and to enjoy his own earnings, is the very foundation stone of . . . freedom," wrote Horace White, the editor of the *Chicago Tribune*. The relationship between employer and employee was simply a contract, and a society based on freely negotiated contracts represented, in their view, the pinnacle of freedom, a great advance over feudalism.[14]

What their economic thinking failed to grasp was that the whole structure of the economy was undergoing radical change. Whereas the early American Republic had been characterized by a continuing labor shortage that kept wages relatively high, the influx of millions of immigrants in the post–Civil War era created a labor surplus. The notion that the laborer had significant negotiating power was simply a convenient upper-class myth. Workers everywhere were being forced to compete and settle for below-subsistence wages. While on average the U.S. economy saw a gradual rise in living standards between the end of the Civil War and the beginning of World War I, nearly half the workforce survived on below-poverty wages. "By the end of the 1880s," wrote David Montgomery in *The U.S. Department of Labor History of the American Worker,* "an income of roughly $500 a year would have been necessary for a family of five in a middle-sized industrial town to enjoy any of life's amenities (newspapers, beer, lodge membership, outings, tobacco) without literally depriving themselves of basic necessities. About forty percent of the working-class families earned less than that." Long periods of unemployment were common, workweeks in excess of fifty hours were routine, child labor was rampant, and health and safety conditions in many workplaces appalling. From 1880 to 1900, an average of thirty-five thousand American workers died each year from work-related injuries and another half million were injured.[15]

Yet taking their bearings from the most extreme laissez-faire versions of the new economic doctrine, the self-styled reformers portrayed government intervention in economic life as nothing less than a violation of natural law. Lincoln had argued that government should actively assist Americans in their quest for economic advancement. It should help to promote equality of opportunity, "clear the path . . . for all." By contrast, the new reformers insisted that the government should have absolutely no role. Godkin's *Nation* preached a particularly simplistic and rigid view of the laissez-faire dogma. In the words of the historian John C. Sproat, "Godkin reduced liberalism to a few simple maxims about society and the economy: wages and prices seek their natural levels when left alone;

society and government can exert no direct control over the individual; poverty and economic suffering result only from the shortcomings of the individuals they afflict."[16]

The notion that one's economic fortunes were connected with one's character—one's hard work, one's thrift, one's persistence and dependability—ran strong in the American bloodstream throughout the nineteenth century. The theme had its origins partly in the old Calvinist idea that good economic fortunes were a sign of God's favor, a visible symbol of belonging to the elect. It was also an outgrowth of individual experience, since many, like Lincoln, found that hard work did enable them to get ahead. But with the dawn of the Gilded Age, this belief was transmuted from Lincoln's message of hope into a verdict of condemnation. It became a rationale for blaming laborers for their desperation and condemning the working poor for their very poverty. Meanwhile, any government effort to intervene on workers' behalf was to be fiercely resisted as a violation of natural law. Proposals for legislation to mandate an eight-hour workday "threatened the very foundation of civilization." Even laws forbidding child labor were anathema. Godkin editorialized against a proposal for a New York state constitutional amendment forbidding employment in factories of children under ten. The government, wrote Godkin, might as well "tell us what to eat, drink, avoid, hope, fear, and believe."[17]

It was precisely the hard-heartedness of these economic doctrines that the nineteenth-century English novelist Charles Dickens had satirized in *Hard Times* (1854) and other works.[18] Partly in response to the critiques of Dickens and others, British policy by the mid–nineteenth century was already moving away from the laissez-faire model toward the beginnings of a modern welfare state. Meanwhile, America's intellectuals, hav-

ing adopted laissez-faire as their own, were codifying an un-
usually harsh and uncompromising version of the doctrine.

Social Darwinism

The harsh version of laissez-faire thinking was made harsher
by yet another development of nineteenth-century thought.
On the eve of the American Civil War, in 1859, Charles Darwin
published his opus *The Origin of Species*.[19] Darwin's new theory of evolution marked perhaps the most important revolution in scientific thought since Copernicus or Isaac Newton. It
utterly transformed the way human beings viewed nature. Just
as Newton's mechanics in the seventeenth century had been
eagerly taken up by political thinkers such as Thomas Hobbes,
who adapted Newton's paradigm to fashion a new, supposedly
scientific theory of the state, so thinkers of the Victorian era
found Darwin's new paradigm of evolution an irresistible lens
through which to explore and reevaluate the age's social and
economic realities. As Newton's discoveries provided the authority for Hobbes's new vision of political life, so Darwin's insights provided seeming scientific authority for the new social
philosophy, propounded perhaps most energetically by Spencer.
Indeed, even before Darwin had published his tome on evolution, Spencer was fashioning a new political vision that integrated laissez-faire thinking with a concept of historical progress
or evolution. "This law of organic progress," Spencer wrote as
early as 1857, "is the law of all progress. Whether it be in the development of the Earth, in the development of Life upon its
surface, the development of Society, of Government, of Manu-
factures, of Commerce, of Language, Literature, Science, Art,
this same evolution of the simple into the complex, through
a process of continuous differentiation, holds throughout."[20]

Darwin's *The Origin of Species*, published two years later, seemed to many, at least among the American reformers, to lend enormous credence to the social vision Spencer was promulgating. Darwin's new theory of evolution based on natural selection seemed to confirm that Spencer had tapped into the very laws of nature. The new view of society as governed by evolutionary laws became known as Social Darwinism. Spencer's writings enjoyed an enormous vogue in America—in contrast to the more tepid reception they were accorded in Spencer's native Britain.[21]

According to Spencer, human social, political, and economic life, like all organic life, was governed by a universal law of adaptation. Those creatures who successfully adapted to their external conditions survived; those creatures who fail to adapt perished. This process of adaptation produced human progress, an inevitable, entirely natural ascent toward the creation of the ideal man. As noted earlier, Spencer called the engine of progress "the survival of the fittest," a phrase he coined in 1864, later incorporated by Darwin himself into subsequent editions of *The Origin of Species*.[22] In Spencer's view, any interference in the natural human competition for survival—particularly by government—was utterly counterproductive. By exposing the whole society to maladaptation, such government intervention could potentially spell society's destruction. The role of the state was solely the defense of individuality, a scrupulous protection of individual rights and rigid noninterference in economic activity. Those societies that most perfectly did not interfere with the individual's absolute rights to life, liberty, and property would survive and progress; those societies that interfered with these rights would eventually die out.[23]

It followed that any attempt by the state to relieve the unemployed, to guarantee rights of employment, or even to provide charity for impoverished widows and orphans posed a threat to progress. Spencer opposed all aid to the poor. "Pervading all nature," he wrote in *Social Statics* (1851), "we may see at work a stern discipline, which is a little cruel that it may be very kind." He continued,

> The poverty of the incapable, the distresses that come upon the imprudent, the starvation of the idle, and those shoulderings aside of the weak by the strong, which leave so many "in shallows and in miseries," are the decrees of a large, far-seeing benevolence. . . . It seems hard that a labourer incapacitated by sickness from competing with his stronger fellows, should have to bear the resulting privations. It seems hard that widows and orphans should be left to struggle for life or death. Nevertheless . . . these harsh fatalities are seen to be full of the highest beneficence—the same beneficence which brings to early graves the children of diseased parents, and singles out the low-spirited, the intemperate, and the debilitated as the victims of an epidemic.[24]

The laborer struggling with wages below subsistence, the sick and infirm, even impoverished widows and orphans, in short society's millions of "losers"—all were unfit, and the most unfit among them deserved to die so that the race as a whole would prosper. The obvious cruelty of this new modern economic system, Spencer claimed, was actually kindness in disguise.

Godkin took up Spencer's harsh gospel in the *Nation*. The beleaguered laborer should learn to be content with his lot, Godkin wrote, since Nature's law decreed that "the more intelligent and thoughtful of the race shall inherit the earth and have the best time" while the rest must settle for a life that was "on the whole dull and unprofitable."[25] Workers who looked to the government for help were actually violating one of the core principles of democracy.

What is remarkable is how, under the influence of Social Darwinism, the definition of democracy was gradually turning into something approaching its opposite. Repelled by the huddling masses of underpaid laborers, the self-styled reformers even raised questions about the merits of universal suffrage, some of them advocating a return to the old system of voting rights on the basis of property ownership.[26] Such antidemocratic proposals never gained much traction. But they signified a sharp departure from Lincoln's understanding of democracy. Lincoln had regarded the equality posited by the Declaration of Independence as a core democratic value. Increasingly, the reformers and Social Darwinists saw *inequality* as a sign of a healthy democracy, albeit one that now exhibited sharp divisions between the rich and the wretched.

The greatest American proponent of Social Darwinism was the Yale professor and cleric William Graham Sumner, who developed a full-blown political philosophy geared to the American scene. Like Godkin, Sumner had a knack for boiling complex doctrines down to snappy ideological formulae. "Let it be understood," he wrote, "that we cannot go outside of this alternative: liberty, inequality, survival of the fittest; not-liberty, equality, survival of the unfittest. The former carries society forward and favors all its best members; the latter carries society downwards and favors all its worst members."[27] Inequality had become the visible sign of democracy.

Whereas the first generation of reformers had expressed suspicion and contempt for the uncultured Robber Barons, Sumner celebrated the new millionaires as the champions of progress. They were the fittest, and their wealth was an expression of natural law: "The millionaires are a product of natural selection, acting on the whole body of men. . . . It is because they are thus selected that wealth . . . aggregates under their hands. . . . They get high wages and live in luxury, but the bargain is a good one for society." He defended hereditary wealth as essential to progress; any effort to tax it would reduce men to "swine." Poverty, meanwhile, was entirely the product of the individual's moral failings: "Let every man be sober, industrious, prudent, and wise, and bring up his children to do so likewise, and poverty will be abolished in a few generations." Sumner opposed any government intervention to improve the conditions of labor, since such measures would favor the unfit at the expense of the fit.[28]

The Gospel of Wealth

The reformers and the Social Darwinists produced an ideology tailor-made for business interests. Industrial magnates and the business community enthusiastically took up the slogans of laissez-faire—an irony, since at the same time big business lobbied the federal government increasingly energetically for what amounted to millions of dollars in preferential treatment. Federal land grants and loans for the railroads in the tens of millions, high tariffs to protect selected industries, and banking and financial regulations that enabled investors to line their pockets at the expense of the unwitting—such were the policies of the federal government in the Gilded Age. Far

from maintaining a scrupulous laissez-faire or hands-off attitude, the government had its thumb on the scale on behalf of its
richest citizens. Still, despite the contradictions, even the hypoc-
risy, laissez-faire came to reign as a kind of official ideology of
the era. It was, observed the Englishman Bryce in 1888, "the orthodox and accepted doctrine in the sphere both of Federal
and State legislation."[29]

Indeed, the story of Gilded Age politics was the story of
the increasing domination of both political parties by business
interests. President Grant openly hobnobbed with the financial speculator James Fisk and other Robber Barons. The new
Republican program of internal improvements cemented a
new and often corrupt alliance between the party and business
interests, the latter eager to gain access to the government's
millions. The Republican Party in turn increasingly tapped
its rich business friends for the growing sums of money needed
to run modern political campaigns.

The Democrats may have attacked Republicans as the
party of business, but they increasingly interpreted their own
Jacksonian heritage in light of the newfangled laissez-faire
doctrines. While ostentatiously championing the cause of the
common people, they were prepared to do little for them. After
defeating the Republican candidate in 1884, the Democratic
president Grover Cleveland, the darling of the mugwumps,
filled his cabinet with businessmen and corporate attorneys
and, in a wholehearted embrace of laissez-faire views, stood
steadfast against government intervention in the economy. In
words that formed a striking contrast to Lincoln's famous
closing lines of the Gettysburg Address, Cleveland affirmed,
"Though the people support the Government, the Government should not support the people."[30] So much for government "for the people."

Government action on a scale that neither national party was prepared to imagine in the 1870s and 1880s might have helped to rectify the worst abuses and address the growing impoverishment of workers. But the laissez-faire doctrine created a formidable ideological barrier to government action to address the problems of the new industrial economy.

Moreover, the laissez-faire doctrines not only influenced the executive branch and the Congress: they had an even more profound influence on the federal judiciary. As the century wound to a close, even as the states and the federal government slowly began to take action to control the excesses of the railroad magnates and the trusts, the Supreme Court consistently ruled that government-chartered corporations were entitled to the same privileges as individual American citizens. Regulation of corporations was rejected as an unjust attempt to deprive them of "life, liberty, or property without due process of law." In *United States v. E. C. Knight,* the Court ruled that the Sherman Antitrust Act—explicitly designed to prevent unfair restraint of trade and monopolies—could not outlaw monopolies in manufacturing because manufacturing involved interstate commerce only indirectly.[31] The effect was essentially to gut the act.

In 1905, in *Lochner v. New York,* the Court in a similar spirit struck down a New York state law limiting the workweek of bakers to ten hours per day or sixty hours per week. In a famous dissent, Justice Oliver Wendell Holmes, Jr., attempted, without success, to have the Court adopt the point of view that "the Fourteenth Amendment does not enact Mr. Herbert Spencer's *Social Statics.*" It was a reflection of how thoroughly Social Darwinism and doctrinaire laissez-faire thinking had come to permeate American constitutional and legal thinking. "A constitution," Holmes added, "is not intended to embody a particular economic theory."[32] In the course of a generation, American libertarians and Social Darwinists had in effect rewritten the nation's social contract, reinterpreted the country's founding documents as laissez-faire charters enshrining economic freedom as an absolute right of individuals and corporations—empowering the fit to prosper while consigning the unfit to deserved suffering and presumably eventual extinction. In the process, Lincoln's American Dream had all but disappeared. In its place was a new vision.

No one provided a more comprehensive account of this vision than that paragon of industrial magnates Andrew Carnegie. Using every available device in the unfettered nineteenth-century economy to consolidate his power in the steel industry, drive out competition, and hold down wages, Carnegie at his peak had accumulated a fortune in excess of $300 million.[33] In a book published in 1889, he promulgated what he called the "Gospel of Wealth." Carnegie's message was an exhortation to rich industrial magnates to spend their millions in good works for the benefit of society. But what was most noteworthy in Carnegie's new Gospel was his acceptance of the depressed condition of late nineteenth-century industrial workers (conditions that, despite occasional denials, he himself played no small role in creating) as not simply an ugly stage in history, but a permanent fact of nature. It was, observed Carnegie, simply the price society paid for enjoying a greater abundance of inexpensive consumer goods: "The price we pay for this salutary change is, no doubt, great. We assemble thousands of operatives in the factory, and in the mine, of whom the employer can know little or nothing, and to whom he is little better than a myth. All intercourse between them is at an end. Rigid castes are formed."[34]

Carnegie used Spencer's doctrine of the survival of the fittest as the justification for this new condition of society—a condition similar in its "caste" system to the old European aristocracies and the antebellum South and profoundly different from the America that Lincoln had imagined he was fighting to preserve:

> The price which society pays for the law of competition, like the price it pays for cheap comforts and luxuries, is also great; but the advantages of this law are also greater still than its cost—for it is to this law that we owe our wonderful material development, which brings improved conditions in its train. But, whether the law be benign or not, we must say of it, as we say of the change in the conditions of men to which we have referred. It is here, we cannot evade it; no substitutes for it have been found; and *while the law may be sometimes hard for the individual, it is best for the race, because it insures the survival of the fittest in every department. We accept and welcome, therefore, as conditions to which we must accommodate ourselves, great inequality of environment; the concentration of business, industrial and commercial, in the hands of a few; and the law of competition between these, as being not only beneficial, but essential to the future progress of the race.* Having accepted these, it follows that there must be great scope for the exercise of special ability in the merchant and in the manufacturer who has to conduct affairs upon a great scale. That this talent for organization and management is rare among men

is proved by the fact that it invariably secures enormous rewards for its possessor, no matter where or
under what laws or conditions [emphasis added].[35]

Carnegie's Gospel of Wealth turned Lincoln's American
Dream on its head. Whereas in Lincoln's America, the underlying principle of economic life was widely shared equality of
opportunity, based on the ideals set forth in the Declaration of
Independence, in Carnegie's America the watchword was inequality and the concentration of wealth and resources in the
hands of the few. Whereas in Lincoln's America, government
was to take an active role in clearing the path for ordinary
people to get ahead, in Carnegie's America, the government
was to step aside and let the laws of economics run their
course. Whereas in Lincoln's America, the laborer had a right
to the fruits of his labor, in Carnegie's America the fruits went
disproportionately to the business owner and investor as the
fittest. Whereas in Lincoln's America, the desire was to help all
Americans fulfill the dream of the self-made man, in Carnegie's
America, it was the rare exception, the man of unusual talent
that was to be supported. Whereas in Lincoln's America, the
engine of progress was the laboring of all Americans, in Carnegie's America, the true engine of progress was the industrial
magnate, in effect Carnegie himself. Whereas in Lincoln's America government was to be on the side of the laborer, in Carnegie's America industrial oppression was justified by its capacity to generate an abundance of cheap consumer goods.

In certain respects, Carnegie intended his book of essays
as a critique of the Robber Barons. A frugal Calvinist at heart,
he condemned the conspicuous consumption and ostenta-
tious spending of the superrich of his era and argued for a re-

strained lifestyle on the part of the industrial magnate. Above all, he argued that those who had made vast sums of money had an obligation to return most of it to society in the form of philanthropy. But even here, he diverged sharply from Lincoln, who saw "charities, pauperism, orphanage" as natural responsibilities of government. Carnegie rejected not only any government effort to aid the poor, but also private philanthropy in the form of direct giving. His main philanthropic endeavor was to build libraries—an important contribution, no doubt, but hardly a comprehensive answer for the millions living on below-subsistence wages, to say nothing of society's sick and infirm, widows and orphans.

Not everyone accepted every detail of Carnegie's Gospel. But in its broad themes, it reflected ideas that enjoyed wide social and political acceptance in late nineteenth-century America and would enjoy something of a revival in the twentieth and the twenty-first. At bottom, the Gospel of Wealth combined laissez-faire economics, strict opposition to government intervention in the economy, an acceptance of extreme economic inequality, a bias against labor in favor of the business owner, a vision of the industrialist and investor as the true engine of economic progress, and a belief that government had no legitimate role in building a middle-class future for all hardworking Americans or even in relieving the condition of the poor.

At all events, Carnegie willy-nilly had hit on a phrase that aptly summarized the dominant ethos of the Gilded Age. Yet even as Carnegie issued his Gospel, the nation was becoming increasingly uneasy with the conditions he described as being so beneficial. Political leaders were gradually coming to grips with the darker legacy of industrial development and beginning to consider and fashion reforms. But support for the Gospel of Wealth would not cease to be one important side of the debate. For decades to come, the struggle over government's economic policy would essentially boil down to the question, which was the true vision of America, the Gospel of Wealth or the American Dream?

Chapter IV
The Age of Reform

The first stirrings of real economic reform in the last decades of the nineteenth century came not from above—from the editorial offices and ivory tower classrooms of the self-professed reformers—but rather from below—from the victims of the new industrial order: the farmers, the industrial workers, and the small business owners and consumers who were being exploited by the railroads and the trusts.

The earliest laws to address the era's economic abuses were enacted at the state level. Gradually, the concerns occupying state governments percolated upward to the U.S. Congress. As the century moved toward its final decade, Congress passed two important pieces of legislation, the Interstate Commerce Act (1887) and the Sherman Antitrust Act (1890). As practical solutions to the problems they addressed, both laws amounted to watered-down compromises, half-measures, indeed, barely more than window dressing. But an important threshold had been crossed. The federal government was now officially in the business of regulating the economy for the benefit of the American public.

Simultaneously, the social conscience of the urban professional classes began slowly to awaken from the dogmas of the Gospel of Wealth. A new generation of writers, including such figures as Henry Demarest Lloyd, Henry George, and Edward Bellamy, focused on the growing inequalities and economic abuses of the era and called for new taxation and government action to regulate industry. Bellamy's novel *Looking Backward from 2000–1887* (1888), which pictured a future utopian society freed from the poverty and inequities of the Gilded Age, sold over a million copies. Its importance, like that of many other writings of the new generation of thinkers, was to challenge the notion that the inequalities and injustices that Americans saw around them were permanent, unchangeable facts of nature—as Spencer, Sumner, Carnegie, and the other Social Darwinists were insisting. Bellamy and the new generation of writers helped a growing literate public to imagine the possibility of constructive social and political change. By the 1890s, Protestant clerics across the North—figures like George Washington Gladden and Walter Rauschenbusch—were adding their voices to the cry against injustice, countering Carnegie's Gospel of Wealth with a Social Gospel that stressed biblical admonitions about the need to care for the poor. In the same years, a new generation of reformers emerged at the state and local levels, both to minister to the needs of the urban downtrodden and to campaign for laws to combat the worst consequences of the new industrial order.[1]

The novelist William Dean Howells, a former writer for the *Nation* with good standing among Godkin and the reformers, privately wrote to the novelist Henry James of his growing misgivings about the direction the country was taking: "I'm not in a very good mood with 'America' myself," Howells wrote in 1888. " . . . After fifty years of optimistic content with 'civilization' and its ability to come out all right in the end, I now abhor it, and feel that it is coming out all wrong in the end, unless it bases itself anew on a real equality." Howells was in frequent contact with the former president Rutherford B. Hayes, who was increasingly disturbed by the same growing inequality in wealth that Howells deplored. "The question for the country now," Hayes wrote in his diary in early 1886, "is how to secure a more equal distribution of property among the people. There can be no republican institutions with vast masses of property permanently in a few hands, and large masses of voters without property. To begin the work, as a first step, prevent large estates from passing, by wills or by inheritance or by corporations, into the hands of a single man." Hayes, a staunch Ohio Republican and former Union general whose political sentiments harked back to Lincoln, was becoming an advocate of an estate tax.[2]

Reforms were also spearheaded by a new generation of college-educated women who turned their efforts to social services. In 1889, Jane Addams, an 1882 graduate of Rockford College, founded Hull House in Chicago with fellow alumna Ellen Gates Starr. Located in a neighborhood brimming with immigrants, Hull House offered a kindergarten, day care, and other services to residents. Florence Kelley joined Hull House and conducted investigations of Chicago's notorious child labor sweatshops. By 1893, she had persuaded Illinois's reform-minded governor John Peter Altgeld and the General Assembly to adopt laws regulating child labor and mandating inspections.[3]

The Ohio governor and former congressman William McKinley, who early in his legal career had taken the case pro bono of thirty-three miners imprisoned for rioting—winning acquittal for all but one—established a state board of arbitration in the early 1890s to help settle labor disputes. He also signed legislation imposing fines on business owners who tried to prevent their workers from unionizing. Forced to call out the army against violent Ohio miners in 1894, he nonetheless led a private charity effort from the governor's mansion to relieve the same miners during the starvation year of 1895. He was widely regarded as a friend of labor, a key factor in his victory in the presidential election of 1896.[4]

Whatever laissez-faire taboo may have existed against the enactment of economic regulation at the federal level, it was increasingly being worn away by the states. At the federal level little attention was paid to economic regulation not only because few national politicians envisioned any role for the federal government in regulating the economy, but also because the two national parties were preoccupied with what they considered much more momentous issues of the day: gold and tariffs.

A national debate over gold and tariffs certainly had important economic implications. But in the 1880s and 1890s, these issues functioned, at a political level, mainly as symbolic substitutes for the real problems occupying the nation: the concentration of economic power in the hands of the trusts and the Robber Barons, the increasing division between the wealthy and the rest of society, and the widespread suffering of the laboring classes. Gold and tariffs became the symbolic focus of a growing class conflict. Democrats increasingly saw the gold standard and high tariffs as symbols of a government that had come to favor business, wealth, and privilege over the mass of citizens. The Republican McKinley was able to counter the Democratic platform with a Republican vision of growing prosperity—"the full dinner pail"—based on sound money (the gold standard), protective tariffs, and high wages for American workers vis-à-vis their oppressed foreign counterparts. In the end, McKinley won both this argument and the election of 1896.

McKinley's opponent in the election of 1896, Williams Jennings Bryan was the era's most famous opponent of the unequal economic consequences of the Gilded Age. A former congressman from Nebraska and one of the nation's most eloquent and fiery orators, Bryan accused the Republican Party of practicing what would later be called trickle-down economics: "The sympathies of the Democratic Party . . . are on the side of the struggling masses who have been the foundation of the Democratic Party. There are two ideas of government. There are those who believe that, if you will only legislate to make the well-to-do prosperous, their prosperity will leak through to those below. The Democratic idea, however, has been that if you legislate to make the masses prosperous, their prosperity will find its way up through every class which rests upon them."[5]

Bryan was the first to frame compellingly what would emerge as a major theme of the twentieth-century Democratic Party. Indeed, his contrast, in effect, between trickle-down and trickle-up economics almost anticipated the modern debate between supply-side and demand-side economists. In certain respects, one could argue that Bryan's vision looked back to Lincoln, at least in favoring the interests of the ordinary worker. But perhaps reflecting the conditions of his age, Bryan's vision was inherently more divisive and less inclusive than Lincoln's, embodying a rhetoric of class conflict quite alien to Lincoln's outlook.

Indispensable to McKinley's electoral success against Bryan was his reputation—dating from his early career and his governorship—as a friend of labor. Kevin Phillips has argued that almost no other Republican could have beaten Bryan in 1896, certainly as decisively, since no other candidate could have escaped the Republican Party's increasingly obvious stigma as the party of big business. Despite his close connection with the rich Ohio business heir Mark Hanna, who shrewdly managed his political campaigns, McKinley was able to build a coalition knitting together the urban workers of the North and the very business owners who were, more often than not, exploiting them. It was an odd union, but like many of his fellow Ohio Republicans, McKinley believed strongly that business and labor had, at bottom, powerful interests in common. Like Ohio's Hayes, his former commander and mentor since Civil War days, McKinley was one of the party's "Lincoln men."[6]

Nonetheless, McKinley's approach, as a politician and a leader, meant almost inevitably that the issues dividing the nation—the trusts, the growing economic inequality of the wealthy and the rest of society, the plight of labor—would remain unaddressed, at least for a time. McKinley was no visionary. He was a well-liked, technically astute, pragmatic, consensus-building politician who got his way through subtle persuasion rather than flaming oratory. As both congressman and governor, he had accomplished much, but always without fanfare. A key to holding the Republican labor–business coalition together lay in McKinley's ability to finesse the obvious conflict of interests between these two groups—to act on labor's behalf, especially as governor, without alienating the business interests that controlled his party. He succeeded by deemphasizing, rather than emphasizing, ideology.

The Bully Pulpit

During the 1880s and 1890s, while national political debate remained focused on gold and tariffs, popular journalism and literature increasingly dwelt on the injustices, corruption, and abominable conditions of life under the new industrial economy. In the 1880s, Henry Demarest Lloyd published a series of exposes in the *Atlantic Monthly* and the *North American Review* detailing business and political corruption. His book *Wealth and Commonwealth* traced the predations of John D. Rockefeller in creating the Standard Oil Trust. The photographer-journalist Jacob Riis's *How the Other Half Lives* presented a jolting portrait of life in the New York tenements, while Stephen Crane's novel *Maggie: A Girl of the Streets* offered a searing fictional portrayal of the same urban world. William Dean Howells's novel *Annie Kilburn* described the evil effects of industrialism in a New England town. His controversial utopian tale *A Traveler from Altruria* satirized the abuses of the era. A swelling chorus of articles in popular magazines and newspapers held a mirror up to industrialized America and showed the urban managerial and professional classes images that increasingly appalled them.[7]

McKinley's successor, Theodore Roosevelt, was the first president and arguably the first national politician to give voice to this rising new national consciousness. Bryan had championed the ordinary laborer, but his biblically tinged populist rhetoric had resonated mainly with the farmers and the rural poor of the West and South. Roosevelt, scion of a wealthy New York City family, former governor of New York State, and the youngest man to assume the nation's highest office, spoke in a language that the citizens of America's urban North could better understand.

Whereas McKinley worked by quietly building consensus, Roosevelt painted in bold public strokes. He famously called the presidency a "bully pulpit" (the word "bully" being slang for "great" or "wonderful"), and he used it in this fashion. In his first State of the Union message, issued less than three months after McKinley's assassination, he finally put in words what had been on the nation's mind for over a decade. "The tremendous and highly complex industrial development" of recent years, he noted, "brings us face to face . . . with very serious problems." The "old laws, and the old customs . . . once quite sufficient to regulate the accumulation and distribution of wealth" were "no longer sufficient."

Roosevelt was careful to hedge his proclamation to avoid an appearance of fomenting class conflict or advocating socialism. "Fundamentally," he stated, "the welfare of each citizen, and therefore the welfare of the aggregate of citizens which makes the nation, must rest upon *individual* thrift and energy, resolution, and intelligence" (emphasis added). Neither was he willing to categorically condemn the Robber Barons: "The captains of industry . . . have on the whole done great good to our people." He cautioned against measures that would sap individual initiative in business; and he noted that regulation of business could be "mischievous." He denied wishing to pit one social group against another. "All this is true," he added, "and yet it is also true that there are real and grave evils." "There is a widespread conviction in the minds of the American people that the great corporations known as trusts are . . . hurtful to the general welfare."

He went on to set forth an agenda bold in both principle and detail. He called for the federal government to "assume power of supervision and regulation over all corporations doing interstate business" and asked for amendments to strengthen the Interstate Commerce Act. He proposed the creation of a new cabinet secretary for commerce and industry with jurisdiction over commerce and labor matters. He called for reform of the government's labor policies, including legislation to limit women's and children's labor hours and a factory law for the District of Columbia. He praised the labor movement and

suggested that government action would be necessary to protect unions—though, significantly, he stressed that labor regulation was still primarily a matter for the states rather than the
federal government. He proposed measures for environmental
conservation and outlined an assertive foreign policy, including a proposal to move forward with the Panama Canal.[8]

Roosevelt well understood the power of his presidential
statements, his bully pulpit. His rhetoric would prove as important as his policies. His new tone and vision had a galva-
nizing effect on the nation. His statements, echoing the feelings
of an increasingly worried and conscience-stricken middle class,
unleashed the pent-up energies of a whole generation of ide-
alists and crusaders. The pace of journalistic and fictional exposes of business and political corruption and labor abuses
quickened noticeably after Roosevelt's State of the Union message in 1901. Several popular magazines, including *Cosmopoli-
tan, McClure's,* and *Collier's,* began devoting an increasing portion of their pages to the writings of those who later would be
called muckrakers (based on a metaphor from John Bunyan's
Pilgrim's Progress used by Roosevelt in a 1906 speech).[9] A series
of new nonfiction and fiction works painted the grim portrait
of the age. Among the most notable were Lincoln Steffens's
The Shame of the Cities (on urban corruption and the political
machines), Ida Tarbell's *History of the Standard Oil Company,*
Frank Norris's novel *The Octopus,* and Upton Sinclair's *The
Jungle.* The writings of the muckrakers in turn built growing
public support for the new policies and laws Roosevelt would
pursue, many of them in his second term, after winning the
election of 1904.[10] Progressivism, as it came to be called, was
becoming the dominant political idea of the age.

In the process, Roosevelt radically redefined the role and
vastly expanded the prerogatives of the federal government.

Taking advantage of the long-dormant provisions of the Sherman Antitrust Act, his administration pursued a series of highly visible prosecutions against the trusts, beginning with a case against the Northern Securities Company in 1902. Federal prosecutors took action against Standard Oil of New Jersey and the American Tobacco Company. In 1906 and 1908—following the publication of Sinclair's *The Jungle,* exposing in gruesome detail the abusive and unsanitary practices in Chicago's meat-packing industry—Roosevelt signed the Pure Food and Drug Act and the Meat Inspection Act, the first real consumer protection legislation. And he also sponsored a series of laws aimed at conservation of the natural environment.[11]

Yet while certainly radical compared with anything that had gone before, Roosevelt's Progressivism still had about it a conservative tenor. His policies were motivated in large measure by a desire to preserve political stability. He was not, like Lincoln, a man of the people. Roosevelt thought like the patrician he was; he acted out of a sense of noblesse oblige. He believed it vital to prevent the nation from splitting asunder into two camps, the rich and the masses. He did not want a country, as he said, "divided into two parties, one containing the bulk of the property owners and conservative people, the other the bulk of the wage workers and less prosperous people generally."[12] Roosevelt's program was a balancing act; he recognized the need to let some of the steam of social resentment out of the pressure cooker of the new industrial economy; but he also wanted, fundamentally, to keep the lid on. He believed he could do this by openly taking the side of the public against the trusts, becoming the public's ombudsman, demanding from business, on behalf of all citizens, what he called a square deal. "Speak softly and carry a big stick," he famously said. But in practice he spoke loudly, with the intention of giving an aggrieved public the sense they had someone in their corner in

Washington who would speak up for them, and not just some-one, but the top fellow.

Roosevelt aimed his reforms primarily at the issues that most troubled the urban managerial and professional classes—the power and abuses of the trusts and the railroads (which often translated into higher consumer prices) and later the safety of consumer food and drugs. On the labor issue, he was less engaged, though his efforts to mediate the Pennsylvania mine strike in 1902, and the pressure he brought directly and indirectly on the mine owners, helped win important conces-sions for the miners.[13]

As time went on, however, Roosevelt was increasingly con-cerned to rein in the enthusiasm that his own rhetoric had un-leashed. He suspected the motives of many of the muckrakers and saw them as stirring up dangerous revolutionary senti-ments. As he wrote to his secretary of war and political heir ap-parent, William Howard Taft, in 1906, "Some of these [writers] are socialists; some of them merely lurid sensationalists; but they are all building up a revolutionary feeling which will most probably take the form of a political campaign. Then we may have to do, too late or almost too late, what had to be done in the silver campaign when in one summer we had to convince a great many good people that what they had been laboriously taught for several years previous was untrue."[14] Roosevelt was looking back to the "economics lessons" that McKinley had given the public during the 1896 campaign to counter Bryan's class warfare based on the "cross of gold."

Yet Roosevelt had also done what McKinley had not dared to do—break with the Republican Party's core business constituency. By the end of his administration, many business-oriented Republicans had had quite enough of Teddy's square deal. The president, observing the tradition since President George Washington of not seeking a third term, tilted his hat to Taft, who easily captured the Republican Party's nomination at the 1908 convention. Taft carried the general election against the Democrats' Bryan almost effortlessly, since by now Roosevelt's Progressivism had effectively stolen much of Bryan's populist thunder. But Taft's administration would be marked by increasingly open warfare between the Republican Party's progressive and conservative wings. Despite having been blessed by Roosevelt, Taft was by temperament far more a creature of the Republican business class, and certainly much less of a maverick, than his colorful predecessor. An avid golfer, the 350-pound Ohioan enjoyed frequenting country clubs, where he hobnobbed pleasantly with the rich.[15] He was not opposed to reform, but his instincts were conservative, and the pace of reform clearly slowed. Perhaps the most important innovations were a lowering of tariff rates (after a bitter fight between free trade progressives and protectionist conservative Republicans), a further expansion of the powers of the Interstate Commerce Commission (including jurisdiction over cable, telegraph, and telephone), and the Sixteenth Amendment, which now authorized the federal government to impose a graduated income tax (previously struck down by the Supreme Court on states' rights grounds).[16]

The rancor between Republican progressives and conservatives was deep enough by 1911–12 that Republican progressives mounted a challenge to Taft, seeking to replace him at the head of the ticket with the progressive senator Robert M. La Follette of Wisconsin. At the national convention, Roosevelt decided to throw his own hat into the ring, effectively elbowing La Follette aside. Taft, however, survived the progressives' challenge and gained renomination. Roosevelt, infuriated, hastily organized a third party. The general election pitted Taft against Roosevelt, now representing the Progressive, or Bull Moose, Party, and the Democrat Thomas Woodrow Wilson, a former Princeton University president who as governor of New Jersey had gained a reputation as one of the nation's leading progressives. Wilson won with 42 percent of the popular vote, while the Democrats retained control of the House and captured the Senate. Together Wilson and Roosevelt had polled 70 percent of the popular vote, Taft just 24 percent. However the election results were read, it was a landslide victory for the Progressive agenda.

Lincoln Redux

Wilson was, in fact, an extraordinary figure. Whether he should be numbered among the nation's greatest presidents remains in dispute among historians. But clearly he was among the most gifted. In America it was unheard of for a former professor to become president. But Wilson broke this mold, and many others. An academic of unusual brilliance—his doctoral dissertation, published as *Congressional Government*, earned him a national reputation at age twenty-eight—he was a former president of the American Political Science Association and an expert and writer on a wide range of subjects. Few presidents have probably had Wilson's keen grasp of the details of policy matters, economic or otherwise. But unlike many a good technical brain, he never lost sight of the larger picture. He was quintessentially a man of vision ("Wilsonianism" today remains almost a synonym for the visionary approach to politics). Perhaps most surprisingly for one whose life had been lived in the shadow of the ivory tower, he was an eloquent orator with an ability to convey his vision—often new, often complex—in language that could quicken the heartbeats of ordinary people.

From the beginning of his career, Wilson was enflamed with the cause of progress and change. His *Congressional Government* recommended sweeping changes in the American political system, challenging the sacrosanct doctrine of the separation of powers and calling on America to move to a parliamentary form of government.[17] As president of Princeton, he attempted to revolutionize the university by sidelining the old boy network of exclusive dining clubs and reorganizing undergraduate education around a college-based system modeled on Oxford. As governor of New Jersey, he presided over a stunning succession of major reforms during a single two-year term. He effectively broke the Democratic political machine that had elected him and pushed through several important new laws: a law creating direct primary voting, a corrupt practices act to curb bribery, an employers' liability law to provide workers' compensation, and a bill establishing a public utilities commission to set rates.[18]

Wilson had genuine insight into politics, and in the campaign of 1912 that insight took him back to Lincoln. What was remarkable was how Wilson's campaign speeches amounted to a self-conscious effort to revive Lincoln's vision of the American Dream. Roosevelt had spoken candidly about social evils and had used federal action and new laws to address many of them. But Roosevelt's perspective on the issues was always a top-down vision, the view of a patrician, of an aristocrat who felt a responsibility for his society out of a sense of noblesse oblige. His emphasis, as noted above, was on preserving the political stability of the country and preventing a descent into class warfare.

Wilson reenvisioned the nation's problems, as it were, from the bottom up. He adopted the perspective of the ordinary citizen, the common worker struggling to manage under the existing conditions of the economy and the political system. Citing Lincoln as a model, he explicitly linked the Progressive agenda to the cause of reviving America's commitment to social mobility and restoring equality of economic opportunity. For Wilson, it was precisely Lincoln's understanding of the meaning of America that needed to be restored. Lincoln, he said, was "a man who rose out of the ranks and interpreted America better than any man had interpreted it who had risen out of the privileged classes or the educated classes of America."[19]

According to Wilson, what had been lost in the Gilded Age—and in the Republican Party—was precisely Lincoln's profound sense that America was about the fate of the average person, about opportunities for the ordinary worker to get ahead. Wilson chided the Republicans for their elitism. "It is amazing," he said, "how quickly the political party which had Lincoln for its first leader,—Lincoln, who not only denied, but in his own person so completely disproved the aristocratic theory,—it is amazing how quickly that party, founded on faith in the people, forgot the precepts of Lincoln and fell under the delusion that the 'masses' needed the guardianship of 'men of affairs.'"[20]

Wilson rejected outright the Gospel of Wealth notion that the industrial magnate was to be revered as the engine of the nation's prosperity: "For indeed, if you stop to think about it, nothing could be a greater departure from original Americanism, from faith in the ability of a confident, resourceful, and independent people, than the discouraging doctrine that somebody has got to provide prosperity for the rest of us."[21]

Lincoln had spoken of the "prudent, penniless beginner." Wilson spoke similarly of the beginner, the man "with only a little capital." But industrial America was no longer Lincoln's America. "American industry is not free, as once it was free," he said. "American enterprise is not free; the man with only a little capital is finding it harder to get into the field, more and more impossible to compete with the big fellow. Why? Because the laws of this country do not prevent the strong from crushing the weak." Like Lincoln, he believed that America needed to be a middle-class nation, and a nation that assimilated beginners to the middle class. There needed to be "the constant renewal of society from the bottom." The "middle class is being more and more squeezed out by the processes which we have been taught to call processes of prosperity," he said. The whole point of American democracy was to provide the humble with access to the American dream, and government should act to ensure this access: "Anything that depresses, anything that makes the organization greater than the man, anything that blocks, discourages, dismays the humble man, is against the principles of progress." This was vintage Lincoln.[22]

The legislative record of Wilson's first term was almost unparalleled, even if history has tended to overlook it, focusing instead on Wilson's entry into World War I, his negotiation of the Treaty of Versailles, and the collapse of his peace plan and the League of Nations after 1919. Yet the list of his domestic achievements was stunning and amounted to a comprehensive new set of government economic policies.

First came tariff reform. Increasingly, progressives had come to see tariff laws as, in effect, a regressive tax on consumers. Notoriously shaped by the efforts of lobbyists, the tariffs protected the trusts from foreign competition and kept prices high. Consumers footed the bill. Legislation during Wilson's first year as president essentially overturned the tariff regime of the nineteenth century, radically reducing rates on hundreds of items (while raising rates on certain luxury goods), and—at the initiative of Representative Cordell Hull—instituted a graduated income tax to provide a new revenue base for the government. In effect, the law shifted the source of federal revenues from a regressive consumption tax in the form of tariffs to a progressive tax on income. In 1916, the tax was significantly raised to cover war preparedness (after U.S. entry into World War I, income taxes were raised again), and for the first time a federal estate tax on large inheritances was established (the latter was a long-standing item on the Progressive agenda, advocated by President Roosevelt as early as 1906). This was both a new technical approach to and a new philosophy of taxation, an effort to gain lower prices through tariff reductions and simultaneously to shift the burden of taxation away from the middle class.[23]

As we have seen, mismanagement of the money supply—and lack of government tools to address the problem—had been a major factor in the raucous boom-and-bust economy of the nineteenth century. Wilson played a key role in crafting the Federal Reserve Act of 1913, which created a sophisticated system for regulating banks and controlling credit and the money supply. The Federal Trade Commission Act of 1914 gave the federal government decisive control over corporate business practices, empowering the commission to require reports from corporations, conduct investigations, and issue "stop and desist" orders to halt illegal practices. The Clayton Antitrust Act expanded prohibitions on monopoly practices and also provided new protections for labor, above all mandating that strikes not be considered acts "in restraint of trade" under the Sherman Antitrust provisions. In addition, laws were passed to require humane conditions for merchant marine sailors, to mandate an eight-hour day for workers on interstate railroads, and to ban from interstate commerce products produced by children under fourteen—though the last was struck down by the Supreme Court.[24]

It is tempting to conclude that the American Dream had made a comeback. Conditions were clearly improving. Once unleashed, the impetus for genuine reform had proved unstoppable. Moreover, Wilson had recovered the essence of the Lincolnian vision and had the words to convey it to his fellow citizens. Ironically, the torch had been passed from Lincoln to Wilson and the Democrats, who now boasted a comprehensive agenda to support their long-standing claim to the mantle of champion of the common people. America was on the road to recovery. But Europe was already engulfed in a war that proved to be more terrible than America's own bloody civil conflict of fifty years earlier. In 1916, Wilson campaigned on a platform of strict isolationism. "He Kept Us Out of War" was the slogan of his campaign. But in 1917, America under Wilson's leadership would plunge headlong into Europe's struggle. Once again war would derail progress toward a "more perfect union," hardening hearts and inducing in Americans a fresh bout of amnesia about the true meaning of Lincoln's American Dream.

Under Woodrow Wilson's leadership, war became the last great cause of the Progressive movement, and it proved to be the movement's undoing. By 1919, when the president returned from Paris with the Treaty of Versailles and his elaborate plan for a League of Nations, the public was sick to death of war and equally weary of Wilson's seemingly inexhaustible store of idealistic rhetoric. As long as Wilson's vision remained focused on improving the lives of ordinary Americans, the public stood behind him. War in the name of an abstract idea of human progress, however, left a bitter taste.

America's direct involvement in World War I had been comparatively brief—eighteen months from early April 1917 to early November 1918. But the disruption of national life had been considerable. Selective Service, enacted in 1917, required over 24 million men to register for the draft. Overnight, the U.S. armed forces swelled from their prewar level of 200,000 to some 2.9 million men. Two million of these shipped off to Europe; 1.4 million saw battle. Over 116,000 perished from combat and disease, while another 200,000 were wounded. At home, the government had seized control of much of the economy. The newly introduced income tax was raised to unprecedented levels.[25]

The impact of the war on economic life was substantial. War production was rapidly ramped up, producing a sharp spurt of growth in 1918. The end of government spending on the military in 1919 was followed by months of recession, succeeded in turn by a true depression. Moreover, by 1920, prices had doubled over their 1914 levels, while incomes had failed to keep pace. Unemployment was rising—peaking at 12 percent (some 5 million workers) in 1920.[26] The public was fed up.

Chapter V
The Business of America Is Business

Republicans correctly gauged the public mood and hit on an apt theme for the election of 1920: normalcy. "Not heroism, but healing," said the Republican candidate, Warren G. Harding, "not nostrums, but normalcy."[1] The swipe at Wilson's rhetorical grandiosity (dismissing it as so many "nostrums") struck a powerful chord. Harding, an affable but otherwise unremarkable senator from Ohio, trounced the Democratic candidate, Governor James M. Cox of Ohio, winning sixteen million votes to Cox's nine million. In certain respects, Harding's postwar administration harked back to President Ulysses S. Grant's administration following the Civil War. It would be remembered mainly for a string of spectacular scandals. Mercifully, perhaps, the president died of a sudden stroke in August 1923 before the malfeasance had come to light. The real importance of the Harding administration was to usher in twelve years of unabashed pro-business Republican rule—a revival of laissez-faire economic doctrine and a return to the Gospel of Wealth.

This time the public embraced the Republican probusiness approach with unparalleled fervor. The reason was simple: it seemed to work. The 1920s were a decade of dramatic economic growth and unprecedented rise in the living standards of most Americans. From 1921 through 1929, Gross National Product (GNP) expanded at an estimated real rate of 4.5 percent per year—well above the average annual growth rates of 3.1 percent per year we have seen since World War II. Once again, the American landscape was transformed. In the nineteenth century, the engines of technological change had been the railroads and steam power. In the 1920s, they were the internal combustion engine and electricity. Within a very few years, the automobile reigned as the new symbol of American life. Between 1919 and 1929, cars on the American road more than tripled, from fewer than 8 million to nearly 27 million, almost one automobile for every household in the nation. Miles of paved road nearly doubled, from 350,000 in 1919 to 662,200 in 1929. By 1929, two-thirds of homes had electricity, and 40 percent had telephones. A proliferation of new "labor-saving devices" filled the household—washing machines and vacuum cleaners, even some refrigerators, to say nothing of those modern marvels, the phonograph and the radio. A host of new products emerged. The modern retail chain store took shape. "You can't lick this Prosperity thing," quipped the comedian Will Rogers late in the decade. "Even the fellow that hasn't got any is excited over the idea."[2]

Yet many of the forces that helped create the new prosperity would also lead to its catastrophic undoing. Chief among these was an economic force whose power to enliven or strangle an economy would only begin to be understood several years after the shock of the Great Crash and the onset of the Great Depression: the level of consumer demand. Historians have cited many factors in attempting to explain the prosperity of

the Roaring Twenties. Clearly, the internal combustion engine
and the advent of electricity—as mainstays of a new technological revolution—played a critical role. Republicans' probusiness policies, which deliberately encouraged business risk
taking (as we shall see later), played some part. But to a degree
that historical commentary often fails to reflect, the boom
of the 1920s was in essence demand driven. The rapidly expanding demand within the U.S. economy had its source in a
startling new phenomenon: widespread borrowing by American consumers.

Buy Now, Pay Later

In 1919, General Motors Corporation established a financial
arm, the General Motors Acceptance Corporation (GMAC), to
enable customers to buy GM cars on installment. It was a fate-
ful decision, with revolutionary implications not only for the
automobile industry, but also for the American economy as a
whole. Installment buying was not an entirely new phenomenon. The Singer Sewing Machine Company had pioneered installment plans to sell sewing machines as early as 1850. By the
turn of the century, pianos and furniture were often sold this
way. In the war years, a handful of small finance companies
sprang up to satisfy the apparently insatiable desire of even
cash-pressed consumers to own automobiles. But until the end
of World War I, installment buying had been largely confined
to lower-income consumers, and it carried a social stigma.
GM's creation of GMAC changed all that. Overnight, installment buying became a middle-class passion. Indeed, consumers
at all levels—except the most wealthy—took advantage of installment buying to acquire cars and eventually the host of new
consumer durables produced by America's "second industrial
revolution."[3]

"Now it's easy for us to get our car," read the headline of a magazine advertisement for Chevrolet in 1925. The ad pictured an attractively attired middle-class couple seated at a desk with a businesslike young salesman in the showroom, happily arranging their automobile financing, while their shiny new Chevrolet shimmered in the background.[4] GM had done something brilliant. The company had found a way to give consumers the money with which to purchase its automobiles—and to charge consumers for the money they had been lent. The system obviously increased GM's profit per sale: not only did the company pocket the margin for the actual sales transaction; it also collected handsome interest on the financing. Most important, GM had found a way to *create* the demand for its product. GM's strategy set a new tone for American business. "Build a better mousetrap," Ralph Waldo Emerson had said, "and the world will beat a path to your door." Such had been the nineteenth-century conviction. But twentieth-century American business was no longer waiting passively for the customer to appear in the doorway. It was going out and roping customers in. The strategy of American business shifted from one of merely selling products to one of actively nurturing, shaping, and, where possible, creating consumer demand on a mass scale.

Advertising itself played a crucial role in this process. The 1920s saw the birth of advertising in its modern form. Its hallmark was often the direct use of emotion to foster demand for products and services. "They Laughed When I Sat Down at the Piano—But When I Began to *Play!*" So read the headline of one of the era's most famous and successful ads—for a correspondence course purporting to teach customers how to play the piano. "I still believe that one can learn to play the piano by mail and that mud will give you a perfect complexion," Zelda Fitzgerald, the novelist F. Scott Fitzgerald's wife, observed wryly after the boom was over.[5] In combination with installment buying, advertising helped foster a culture of competitive acquisition, a true consumer economy.

Advertising also contributed to the political mood of the age. It sold the Gospel of Wealth—even to those for whom prosperity was, in Will Rogers's words, more an idea than a reality, a mere dream. Installment buying put the new luxuries of the second industrial revolution within reach of people who, by earlier standards, could not afford them. Installment buying made the new luxuries suddenly "affordable." The researchers Robert and Helen Lynd, in their famous study of Middletown (their pseudonym for Muncie, Indiana) found that in 1923 nearly half the town's 123 working-class families owned automobiles. Of these 60 families, 26 lived in makeshift shacks, of which 21 lacked even a bathtub. Yet there was their automobile, parked out front.[6]

From the standpoint of economics, the impact of advertising and installment buying was to significantly expand consumer spending—both directly, by putting more (borrowed) money in the hands of consumers, and indirectly, by creating a culture of acquisition in which everybody was expected to own an automobile, a washing machine, a vacuum cleaner, a phonograph, a radio, and so forth. As installment buying spread from automobiles to other consumer durables such as furniture, washing machines, vacuum cleaners, radios, phonographs, jewelry, and even clothes, demand for such items accelerated. By the end of the decade, three-quarters of automobiles and washing machines, some 90 percent of furniture, two-thirds of vacuum cleaners, three-fourths of radio sets, and 80 percent of phonographs were being purchased on installment-based credit.[7]

Between 1919 and 1929, consumer debt nearly tripled, from $2.6 billion to $7.1 billion. Since installment loans in the 1920s typically had a one-year term, the yearly level of consumer debt provided a rough indication of the amount of money being borrowed by consumers to finance their purchases in that year. In 1929, outstanding consumer debt of $7.1 billion equaled more than three-quarters of the total amount that consumers spent on durable goods ($9.2 billion).[8] The manufacturing sector for durables—ranging from automobiles to radios—was increasingly dependent on installment buying for its economic health.

A second sector critically dependent on consumer borrowing was residential construction. Growth in mortgage borrowing for family homes followed roughly the same pattern as installment borrowing, with mortgage debt nearly tripling from $10.1 billion in 1919 to $31.2 billion in 1929. While consumer spending for new houses was not strictly speaking consumption (it is reckoned in National Income and Product Accounts as investment), it played a significant role in the health of the economy. Together durable goods purchases and residential construction amounted to 13 percent of GNP in 1929.[9] But this figure (based on later estimates not available at the time) understates their impact, since both industries drew heavily on commodities and raw materials and therefore had a significant multiplier effect throughout the economy.

Even as American business increasingly embraced what might be termed a demand-side approach—spending increasing millions on advertising and marketing, stoking consumer demand, and financing the demand with installment credit— orthodox economic thinking retained its supply-side bias. As the British economist John Maynard Keynes was later to point out, economic thinking of the era was dominated by Say's Law, named for the classical economist Jean-Baptiste Say, and often summarized by the formulation "supply creates its own demand." "The encouragement of mere consumption is no benefit to commerce," wrote Say. " ... It is the aim of good government to stimulate production, and of bad government to encourage consumption." Government policymakers tended to view production—supply as opposed to demand—as the driving force of the economy.[10] In this respect, the prevailing point of view had changed little since the Gilded Age. In the era of the Robber Barons, the industrial magnate—the producer— was widely seen as the engine of economic progress. Woodrow Wilson had attacked this idea on political grounds, arguing that the view that wealth was created from above was essentially un-American. But in the 1920s, the cult of the businessman returned. Increasingly, the business leader was regarded as the hero of the new prosperity. Free the businessman to unleash his energies and creativity, his productive impulses—so the conventional wisdom went—and all would benefit. This production- and supply-oriented vision of economic life— codified in Say's Law—was the basis for the notion that wealth by nature "trickled down" from above (to use the phrase made famous by Treasury Secretary Andrew W. Mellon). The business magnate was the true font of prosperity. In reality, to a degree that almost no one understood at the time, the prosperity of the 1920s was demand-driven, the product of the newly eager, big-spending, big-borrowing American consumer.

An Economy of Risk

The prosperity of the 1920s was not magic. In essence, it was based on increasing consumer demand heavily financed by consumer borrowing. This was all well and good, as long as prosperity continued on the upswing. But amid the exuberance of the era, it was easy to forget an elementary truth—namely, that borrowing carried risk.

"The business of America is business," affirmed President Calvin Coolidge. The Republican administrations of the 1920s saw their economic mission as one of enabling business to do its job. For government, this meant mainly getting out of the way. Lower taxes. Less regulation. Indeed, virtually no regulation. Business should be helped or otherwise left alone. As business prospered, so would America. From their probusiness perspective, the Republicans saw prosperity coming from the producer, from the top down. "Give tax breaks to large corporations," Secretary Mellon famously said, "so that money can trickle down to the general public, in the form of extra jobs."

Mellon's life story formed a link between the Gilded Age Gospel of Wealth and the cult of prosperity that dominated the Roaring Twenties. The country's third richest man behind John D. Rockefeller and Henry Ford, Mellon hailed from the small circle of Pittsburgh's superrich that had included, among others, Andrew Carnegie, Henry Clay Frick, and George Westinghouse. Carnegie, Andrew Mellon's senior by twenty years, was a friend of the younger Mellon's father, Judge Thomas Mellon, founder of the Mellon family banking fortune. Andrew Mellon, himself, was a close friend and frequent business partner of Frick, Carnegie's young protégé, his successor as chairman of the Carnegie Steel Company, and later a bitter Carnegie rival. Frick was among the most notorious of the Robber Barrons, famous for the execrable labor conditions in his coke plants. Mellon shared the Gospel of Wealth conviction that one's economic circumstances were the product of one's own initiative, and that the key to national prosperity was freeing exceptional individuals to pursue great wealth. "Any man of energy and initiative in this country," he wrote, "can get what he wants out of life. But when that initiative is crippled by legislation or by a tax system which denies him the right to receive a reasonable share of his earnings, then he will no longer exert himself and the country will be deprived of the energy on which its continued greatness depends."[11]

Appointed as secretary of the treasury by Harding, Mellon continued in the post through the subsequent administrations of Presidents Calvin Coolidge and Herbert H. Hoover. As treasury secretary, Mellon's main initiative was a series of tax cuts designed to reduce the wartime income tax rates on the nation's highest-income citizens. He was, in fact, the nation's first supply-side economist, though the term had not yet been coined. Adherents of supply-side economics in more recent years, under Presidents Ronald Reagan and George W. Bush, would later cite Mellon as a progenitor and a hero of the supply-side agenda.

Mellon subscribed to the laissez-faire view that the economy was self-regulating. Downturns might come, of course— the country had seen a bad one in 1920–21—but the economy would self-correct. To be sure, the costs of such episodes were unevenly distributed. The five million ordinary workers left jobless during the depression of 1920–21 paid the steepest price. But that was simply the natural order of things. It was the way the economy worked, and worked best.

The Republicans rejected outright the Progressive Era idea that business required oversight. Probusiness administrators committed to a hands-off posture took the reins of government. William E. Humphrey, Coolidge's appointee as chairman of the Federal Trade Commission (FTC), openly referred to the commission as a "publicity bureau to spread socialistic propaganda." Under Humphrey, the FTC, the federal government's main arm for regulating corporations, was rendered largely toothless. Concern about trusts was discarded. Apparently illegal mergers multiplied while the government remained on the sidelines, with open eyes. "So long as I am Attorney

General," said Harry Daugherty during Harding's administration, "I am not going unnecessarily to harass men who have unwittingly run counter with the statutes." The one area in which the Republicans showed an appetite for activism was in opposition to organized labor. "So long and to the extent that I can speak for the government of the United States," said Daugherty, "I will use the power of government to prevent the labor unions of the country from destroying the open shop." Companies moved against unions with administration blessing, while the Supreme Court handed down a series of defeats for labor's ability to organize. Between 1920 and 1929, labor union membership declined by about 30 percent.[12]

The Republicans' probusiness policies also brought two other by-products. One was quite visible at the time: a growing inequality in income and wealth. The other would come to light only when it was too late: mounting economic risk.

The benefits of the new prosperity were spreading unevenly: the rising tide was failing to lift all boats. According to estimates by the National Bureau of Economic Research, manufacturing productivity (measured in output per hour) grew by almost 50 percent from 1921 through 1929. Manufacturing profits exploded, but little or none of the massive productivity gains were being passed to the nation's approximately ten million industrial workers in the form of higher wages. By 1929 average hourly wages of production workers—at $0.56—instead of advancing from 1921 had actually declined by 15 percent in real terms. Meanwhile, the share of total national income captured by the top 1 percent of earners rose from 12 percent in 1920 to 15 percent in 1929; in 1929, the highest-income 5 percent captured 26 percent of total income, and the highest 20 percent of households were taking in well over half (54 percent) of the nation's entire yearly income.[13]

The effects of risk taking were more subtle, but more catastrophic in the long run. Republicans failed to grasp that in rejecting the idea of regulating business, they were willy-nilly exposing the economy to heightened risk. In the absence of government oversight, businesses engaged in increasingly risky practices. The fact that administration officials continually telegraphed an "anything goes" message to the business community hardly helped. The problem was particularly acute in the booming financial sector. On Wall Street, stock manipulation and insider trading were rampant. Ordinary investors were repeatedly cheated as big investors secretly pooled or coordinated their market activity to push stock prices up or down at will, getting out of a stock before the mass of investors suffered the loss.[14] Brokers, meanwhile, promoted their own especially dangerous form of the installment plan, encouraging investors to buy stocks "on margin." Individuals purchased stocks by paying as little as 10 to 25 percent of their value, essentially borrowing the rest from the stockbrokers. Such high "leveraging" was the essence of risk. An investor who bought a $100 stock by plopping down just $10 stood to double his money if the stock rose to $110. Fine and good. But if the stock fell to $50, he would not only lose his $10 but also be out an additional $40, which he now owed to his broker. Multiply that by 100 shares, and you were talking real money. Outside the stock market, unethical business and accounting practices abounded. Meanwhile, the richest of the rich on Wall Street were failing to pay their fair share. A congressional investigation in 1932 revealed that twenty partners of the nation's leading and most prosperous investment bank, the House of Morgan, had paid not a penny in income tax.[15]

The experience of the 1920s suggests the existence of a "risk-return" trade-off for national economic growth, analogous to the risk-return trade-off for an individual investment. The principle is basic to finance: investments that yield high returns usually carry higher risk; lower-risk investments generally yield lower returns. The Republicans' laissez-faire approach was a potentially high-return strategy, but it also carried terribly high risks that at the time were not at all understood. A more regulated economy—one in which the government played an active oversight role—might produce somewhat lower levels of economic growth; but it also might offer greater insurance against the kind of catastrophe in which the Roaring Twenties culminated: the Great Depression.

Americans for the most part were buoyed by the ride up the 1920s roller coaster; but the ride down was too terrible to forget. Following the stock market crash in October 1929, the American economy descended into a rapid tailspin. By 1932, with twelve million out of work—nearly a quarter of the labor force—tens of thousands of men riding railroad boxcars from town to town in vain search of employment, tens of thousands more living in makeshift tent camps on vacant lots in major cities (popularly named Hoovervilles), countless families across the nation lacking shelter, heat, food, and even shoes and clothing for their children, the risk had simply become unacceptable.[16] Business had taken the risks; now ordinary Americans were paying the terrible price. Overnight, the 1920s land of milk and honey had turned into a biblical land of famine. It seemed as if the Gospel of Wealth had destroyed the American Dream.

Explaining the Depression

At bottom, the forces behind the phenomenon of the Great Stock Market Crash of 1929 are familiar. In the history of finance, they represent a recurring phenomenon. Perhaps the best explanation for the phenomenon lies in a phrase used by Federal Reserve Chairman Alan Greenspan to describe a similar bull market many decades later: "irrational exuberance." The Great Bull Market of 1928–29 was a bubble, not unlike the Tulip Bulb Craze that overtook the Netherlands at the dawn of the seventeenth century or the South Sea Bubble on which many a British fortune foundered in the eighteenth. A few select stocks began rising dramatically in March 1928, as large investors, anticipating a recovery from the 1927 recession, entered the market. Newspapers noticed the climb, and soon everybody was in the market or wanted in. The vast influx of new investors pushed up prices, which in turn raised expectations. Soon the mania was self-reinforcing as the market nearly doubled in a span of sixteen months, and some stocks tripled, quadrupled, or even quintupled in value. By 1928, however, the Federal Reserve was already tightening interest rates, partly to curb the rampant stock speculation. Industrial production was slowing. Stocks had lost their connection with economic fundamentals. A crash—a bursting of the bubble—was inevitable.

Even decades after the event, despite reams of scholarship on the era, the precise causes of the Great Depression that followed the Great Crash remain in dispute. We have witnessed stock market crashes since 1929, without the same subsequent catastrophic effects on the economy, notably in 1987 and 2000. How did the 1929 crash manage to disrupt the entire economy? And why did the economic tailspin continue unabated for years? From the best of recent scholarship, with all the benefits of hindsight, a set of plausible answers has emerged.

Keynes came close to identifying the trigger of the Depression in formulating the concept of "aggregate demand." In his *General Theory of Employment, Interest, and Money* (1936), Keynes successfully challenged the supply-side bias embodied in Say's Law—focusing attention instead on the demand side of the economy. The real driving force in the depression was a sharp drop in consumption, as the economist Peter Temin was able to show decades later, using techniques partially derived from Keynes.[17] Businesses failed to invest in production for a simple reason: they suddenly lacked customers to buy their products.

The general economic downturn in 1930 seems to have resulted from the impact of the market crash on consumer demand. It came via two avenues. First, the rising stocks of the 1920s had produced a "wealth effect" among the upper-income citizens who owned most stocks. As their paper assets rose, stock investors felt freer to spend. In the economy of the 1920s, the new generation of durable goods—from automobiles to vacuum cleaners to refrigerators—was being acquired most avidly and easily by those nearer the top of the income scale. Given that the top 20 percent of earners were taking in more than half the nation's total yearly income, any change in the consumer spending behavior of this group would have a noticeable effect. Particularly because of the practice of buying stocks on margin, many of these individuals had gone from wealth to poverty nearly in a matter of days in October 1929. Almost all had been badly burned. Wealth effect purchasing dried up. Second, and perhaps more important, middle-income consumers had been buying automobiles and other durables on installment. Loans seemed a good bet when the market was booming. The Stock Market Crash suddenly raised questions about the future health of the economy. Consumers became cautious, reluctant to take on new borrowing commitments until the smoke from the stock market disaster cleared.

The impact of the new consumer caution was especially profound in two key sectors, automobile sales and new housing construction, both big-ticket items and both heavily dependent on consumer borrowing. From 1929 to 1930, the number of cars sold dropped by close to 40 percent; the value of new residential housing put in place fell by nearly half.[18] These were catastrophic declines. They occurred precisely in sectors with an especially strong multiplier effect on the rest of the economy.

The goose that had been laying the golden eggs of the 1920s—the American consumer—was suddenly panicked and clammed up.

Ways Out

There were two ways out of the Depression following the Crash and the catastrophic decline in consumption of 1929 and 1930. One was fiscal policy; the other was monetary policy. Neither was fully understood at the time. But it also needs to be emphasized that the reigning economic orthodoxy—the supposedly immutable natural laws underpinning the Gospel of Wealth—formed a major barrier to discovering these solutions. It was this orthodoxy that had to be overcome.

Fiscal policy, based on Keynes's General Theory and developed into a mature theory by later generations of demand-side economists, suggested that the government could resuscitate the economy by using deficit spending to expand "aggregate demand." By plowing new money into the economy, in the form of direct purchases by government of goods and services or wages paid to workers on government projects, the government could expand overall demand and get the economy moving again.

Even if the government in 1930 had understood this fiscal strategy, it would have been hard-pressed to execute it. The reason was simple: the government was just too small. Total federal outlays in 1930 stood at about $3.3 billion, or about 4 percent of GNP. Between 1929 and 1930, GNP had fallen by $12.7 billion—a drop more than three times the size of the entire federal budget. Consumption alone had fallen $7.3 billion—a sum more than twice the total amount of federal spending. Even a substantial percentage increase in the spending side of the small federal budgets of the era would probably have been insufficient to overcome the Depression. Only when government was in a position to engage in a level of deficit spending equal to a significant percentage of GNP would it be in a position to "cure" the economy. This finally occurred decisively in 1942, after America's entry into World War II, when federal outlays jumped to $35.1 billion, or 22 percent of GNP, while the federal deficit rose to $20.5 billion, or 13 percent of GNP.[19] In that year, unemployment fell to 3.1 percent (aided by the fact that nearly four million military personnel were now on the government payroll, being paid for partly by money the government had borrowed).[20]

The point is: the limited government of the 1920s and 1930s was simply too small to manage a massive modern industrial economy through fiscal policy. It was a tiny tugboat unable to steer the *Titanic*. When things went massively wrong, the government was simply too small and inconsequential an economic player for its fiscal policy actions to have much effect.

The other way out was monetary policy. That would have involved greatly loosening credit to put more money in the hands of consumers and producers. If credit became cheap enough, consumers might start borrowing again. Here again the reigning orthodoxy stood in the way—and this time the orthodoxy was enshrined in federal law. A critical element of the Gospel of Wealth, as we have seen, was the belief in "sound money." Sound money meant money based on gold. Sound money was not a terrible idea. It offered excellent protection against inflation (which would pose a major challenge to the American economy in a later era). The problem was that the gold standard severely circumscribed policymakers' control over the money supply and closed off the option of meeting a severe deflation with a major increase in the supply of money. Theoretically, the Federal Reserve Bank might have pursued an aggressive "easy money" policy from 1930 onward. But we were decades away from the monetary theory which would have provided the rationale for such a policy. Moreover, the Federal Reserve was prevented from taking such action by a combination of law and ideology. Federal law required that the Fed have on hand $40 worth of gold for every $100 in circulation. The only way to ensure against a run on gold was to keep interest rates high. (With interest rates high, it was more profitable to collect interest than to cash the dollars in for gold.) But high interest rates and tight money were the last things the economy needed when the aim was to get consumers to spend. The Fed's legal responsibilities were reinforced by an orthodoxy that saw the abandonment of sound money as the prelude to an apocalypse. Ironically, fear of one kind of apocalypse helped bring on another, as the economy sank deeper into its hole.[21] The Fed's tight money policy provided the context for the cascading sequence of thousands of bank failures, beginning in 1930, that turned already panicked consumers into paralyzed catatonics and wiped out the life savings of millions of citizens.[22]

The first casualty of the Depression was the belief that the economy would self-correct, that everything would right itself by the magic of laissez-faire. At first nearly everybody expected a quick recovery, following the pattern of 1920–21.

Businessmen urged consumers to tighten their belts and return to the frugal habits so widely abandoned in the 1920s (it
was the wrong advice: what consumers needed was enough
money to spend). Like many members of the business community, Secretary Mellon believed that periodic recessions
were necessary to purge the economy of inefficiencies. His advice to President Hoover: "Liquidate labor, liquidate stocks,
liquidate the farmers, liquidate real estate."[23] With unemployment already rising to unprecedented levels in 1930, Hoover, to
his credit, understood that such words now had too harsh a
ring for most Americans. The president initially took some
small steps in what economists would later argue was the right
direction, increasing the pace of federal spending for construction and exhorting the states to follow suit. But soon he
reverted to the economic orthodoxy, resisting proposals for
federal relief and attempting instead to encourage state relief
and private charity efforts. As growing unemployment reduced
increasing millions of Americans to insolvency, poverty, home-
lessness, and even starvation, state relief and private charity
efforts were simply overwhelmed.

Economic conditions went from bad to worse. More
than a thousand banks failed in 1930; from 1930 through 1932,
the total would rise to over five thousand. In three years, nearly
$3 billion in deposits were wiped out, the life savings of mil-
lions of Americans. Another nearly $3 billion would go up in
smoke in 1933.[24] Meanwhile, depositors rushed to withdraw
their cash before banks went belly-up. Runs on banks became
commonplace. From 1929 to 1932, the broader measure of the
money supply (M_2, which, roughly speaking, included currency
in circulation as well as money in checking and savings accounts) plummeted by $10 billion, or 22 percent.[25] Money
available for both lending and spending was simply evaporat-

ing, as banks collapsed and consumers hoarded cash; demand was rapidly draining out of the economy.

The irony was pitiful. Millions of tons of grain rotted in elevators as children went hungry. Warehouses remained stocked with goods that no one had the money to purchase. Thousands of factories simply shut down. The vast machinery of plenty, built up over centuries of economic striving and two industrial revolutions, had nearly ground to a halt.

In 1932, Hoover pushed Congress to create the Reconstruction Finance Corporation to provide federal government loans to banks, building and loan associations, and railroads to support construction projects. Here at last was a vehicle for modest fiscal stimulus. But the money was slow in trickling out of Washington, and the usefulness of the measure was undermined by an ill-advised tax increase in the same year (the brainchild of Mellon), which took money out of taxpayers' pockets and further reduced demand.[26]

Chapter VI
The Renewal of the American Dream

Franklin D. Roosevelt, the Democratic nominee in 1932, was no less a captive of economic orthodoxy than the Republicans. During the campaign, Roosevelt attacked the Hoover administration as spendthrift and called for a balanced budget and a reduction in federal spending. In other words, Roosevelt assailed Hoover for just about the only thing he was doing right. After the fact, a supporter of Roosevelt observed, "Given later developments, the campaign speeches often read like a giant misprint, in which Roosevelt and Hoover speak each other's lines."[1]

Yet while sharing some of the orthodox beliefs of the time—in particular, favoring balanced budgets and sound money—Roosevelt departed from the orthodoxy in one critical respect: he believed strongly in the possibility of constructive government action. Roosevelt was a progressive, an heir to the progressive tradition on two different sides: he had served in Woodrow Wilson's administration (as assistant secretary of the navy), and he had married Theodore Roosevelt's niece, the formidable Eleanor. Roosevelt knew from watching Wilson, and for that matter Teddy, that government could be an active instrument of change: it could be used to reshape economic life; it could establish a new and better set of rules for economic activity; it could be a tool for solving problems. It was a tool Roosevelt was fully prepared to use.

Against the relative passivity of the Republicans—a legacy of the long-standing laissez-faire taboo—Roosevelt proposed a bold course of government action. The byword of his approach was experimentation. "It is common sense to take a method and try it," he said. "If it fails, admit it frankly and try another. But above all, try something."[2]

"Try something." The words spoke directly to the public mood. Do something, anything, to halt the slide into economic apocalypse. At the Democratic National Convention, Roosevelt pledged "a new deal for the American people." "New Deal" became the slogan of his administration and the synonym for a revolution in federal government policy.

Missing Macroeconomics

Interestingly, FDR's New Deal did not really solve the problem of the Depression, or it did so only slowly and partially and more often by happenstance than by design. Although unemployment gradually fell from its peak of 25 percent in 1933, unemployment remained in the double digits for nearly the entire decade. While reliable official unemployment statistics were not available at the time (the government would only begin to track unemployment reliably in 1942), the fact that even by the end of the decade the economy had not yet returned to a state of prosperity was plain for all to see.

The immediate problem besetting the economy in the 1930s was essentially macroeconomic. The source of the economy's weakness lay in the collapse of demand, and especially consumer demand. The Roosevelt administration never developed anything approaching systematic fiscal or monetary policies to address this core macroeconomic issue. One reason was lack of knowledge about how the economy worked: the conceptual tools for positive macroeconomic policies had not yet been developed. Only in 1936 would John Maynard Keynes publish his *General Theory,* and it would take the economics profession and policymakers a few years to absorb the lessons of Keynes's new understanding. Keynes actually met with Roosevelt in 1934 and attempted to encourage the president to engage in more deficit spending. But the meeting was abortive on both sides. "He left a whole rigmarole of figures," Roosevelt remarked to his labor secretary, Frances Perkins, after the session. "He must be a mathematician rather than a political economist." For his part, Keynes was surprised at FDR's lack of economic comprehension. Keynes "supposed the President was more literate, economically speaking," he told Perkins.[3]

In fact, monetary remedies came more promptly than fiscal steps—though again this was a matter almost of politics rather than economic policy. In Congress, "soft money" men of the William Jennings Bryan tradition were gaining ground, while some financial experts were also calling for "reflation." In April 1933, Senator Elmer Perkins of Oklahoma attached an amendment to the farm bill that would effectively take the United States off the gold standard, by authorizing expansion of the currency through monetization of silver and printing of greenbacks. Sensing the winds of political change, Roosevelt was gradually relinquishing his commitment to "sound money." The president agreed to the amendment in modified form.

From a macroeconomic standpoint, Roosevelt's abandonment of the gold standard in 1933 may have been the most important single policy measure setting the American economy on a path to recovery—though there is little evidence that the president fully understood this. Interestingly, even so conservative a financial authority as J. P. Morgan saw the positive implications of this step, publicly signaling his approval at the time.[4] The new law freed the Federal Reserve Banks to pursue an easier money policy, pointing a way out of the killing credit crunch that was choking the economy nearly to death. The New York Federal Reserve Bank immediately lowered its discount rate from 3.5 to 3 percent in April and dropped it to 2.5 percent in May. The rate would fall to 1.25 percent by February of the following year. April 1933, the month the United States abandoned the gold standard, marked the first month since August 1929 in which the American economy actually experienced growth. By 1934 the money supply was expanding again, though ever so slowly.[5] In a technical economic sense, the Depression could even have been said to have ended—since the contraction had hit its trough—but in reality the expansion would be so slow that recovery would feel like a continuing Depression for many years to come.

How do these Depression-era measures compare with policies pursued in more recent times? The pace of interest rate reductions by the New York Fed in 1933–34 (with other Federal Reserve Banks generally following suit) resembled the aggressive easy money policy pursued in 2001–02 by Federal Reserve Chairman Alan Greenspan immediately following the onset of recession in March 2001, a year following the technology stock bust. At the first signs of recession, the Fed in April 2001 began lowering interest rates at a comparable though slightly faster pace than the rate cuts in 1933–34 (Greenspan also continued the process, ultimately taking rates even lower than the rates of the 1930s central bankers).[6] The result in 2001–02 was a shallow, fairly short recession. As the success of Greenspan's policies tended to confirm, easier money could have been the right medicine for the American economy during the Great Depression. But the first steps toward easier money in the 1930s came very late in the course of the disease. During the forty-three months before April 1933, the U.S. economy had been allowed to dig itself into too deep a hole. It would take years to climb out.

As for fiscal policy, there is no evidence that Roosevelt made conscious use of deficits to increase overall demand, or that he was in any measure influenced by Keynes's new macroeconomic ideas. The federal government did run substantial deficits; they grew willy-nilly as a result of the panoply of new federal programs Roosevelt was putting in place. Between 1932 and 1936, the federal deficit rose from $2.7 to $4.3 billion—the peak deficit for the prewar years. But the dollar increase in federal deficit spending only amounted to about 1 percent of GNP over four years, a figure probably insufficient to affect the economy significantly.[7] In addition, whatever minor stimulant effect the increased federal spending might have had was largely canceled out by tax hikes at the state level. As the states battled to eliminate their budget deficits, they increased annual revenue collection between 1932 and 1936. As the federal government was putting more money into the economy, the states were taking more out via taxation, partly to reduce their deficits. Much of what came in one door went out the other.[8]

In addition, Roosevelt, still probably believing in balanced budgets, pursued a series of un-Keynesian tax increases in 1935, 1936, and 1937 that doubled federal revenues as a share of GDP, from 3 to 6 percent. These tax increases had the effect of rapidly reducing the federal deficit from over 5 percent of GNP in 1936 to well under 1 percent of GNP in 1938.[9] This budget balancing might have seemed a good thing to a certain orthodox cast of economic mind. But the effect of reducing deficits was to *shrink* aggregate demand. Instead of putting borrowed money into the economy, the federal government was now taking money out. Indeed, Roosevelt's tax increases were probably a factor in the onset of a second deep recession in 1937–38. Clearly, whatever else he may have been doing, FDR was not using fiscal policy or deficits to manage the economy in the modern sense of that term.

The New Deal

What, then, was the significance of the New Deal? In the first place, the psychological impact of Roosevelt's leadership is not to be underestimated. By 1932, depression was not merely an economic phenomenon; it was an apt description of the country's state of mind. Roosevelt's easy optimism, self-confidence, and bold experimental spirit instilled hope, and hope was a vital ingredient of recovery. The famous line from FDR's first inaugural—"The only thing we have to fear is fear itself"— was not just a masterful piece of rhetoric. It was also an economic analysis. The nation had been thrown off its horse. To move forward, people had to find the gumption to climb back into the saddle again. The country had absorbed the full brunt of risk inherent in a modern economy. But for modern economic life to go forward, Americans had to be persuaded to begin taking risks once again: the risk of spending, the risk of investing, the risk of borrowing, and for that matter the risk of putting one's money in a bank. If Americans who had money decided to sew most of it up in their mattresses—as some were doing and others were tempted to do—the modern economy was finished. There could be no economic life without risk, yet somehow the human consequences of that risk had to be reduced and distributed more equitably. Americans had remained relatively unfazed by the growing income inequality of the 1920s. What they found intolerable after 1929 was the unequal distribution of the terrible consequences of economic risk.

This was in a certain sense the central significance of the New Deal and its most enduring legacy—though New Dealers would probably not have described it in precisely such terms. The most enduring programs of the New Deal were designed to wring extreme risk out of the economy and to ensure that whatever risk remained was distributed more equitably among all segments of the population. Its major tools were *regulation* and *insurance.* Roosevelt sought to use regulation to prevent business from taking undue risks (and engaging in corrupt practices) of the kind that had brought on the stock market crash. At the same time, he sought to put in place social insurance programs—such as unemployment insurance and Social Security—to protect ordinary Americans from the worst perils of modern economic life. The two measures, regulation and insurance, were mutually reinforcing. While regulation may have reined in business, the combination of regulation and insurance instilled consumer confidence, especially in banks and financial institutions, in a sense gradually giving business back the customers who had fled when the roof came crashing in. By reducing or eliminating irresponsible business risk taking and by providing ordinary Americans with an insurance policy against the worst economic misfortunes, FDR rewrote the

American social contract in a way that preserved the free market economy, opened the way to continued prosperity, and protected the American Dream.

This is not to discount the importance of the many direct relief programs put in place by the Roosevelt administration—the Civilian Conservation Corps, the Civil Works Administration, the Public Works Administration, and later the Work Projects Administration, and so on. One critical effect of these federal investment and public works programs was to lower unemployment. It is a little-known fact that later statistics developed by the scholar Stanley Lebergott and the Bureau of Labor Statistics—and usually treated as the official estimates for unemployment during the era—counted the millions employed in federal public works projects as part of the *unemployed* (they were thought to be in temporary employment). By the mid- to late 1930s, there were 2 to 3.5 million such "emergency workers" on the federal payroll, which meant that real unemployment was actually 4 to 7 percent lower than the numbers the bureau has provided. The direct relief programs should not be dismissed: they created jobs for millions of breadwinners and incomes for millions of families who otherwise might have been hard-pressed to survive. Nonetheless, even counting the public works laborers as employed, unemployment remained in double digits for the rest of the decade, with the sole exception of 1937, when it stood at over 9 percent. As late as 1940, nearly a tenth of the workforce (9.5 percent) remained unemployed.[10]

After declaring a four-day bank holiday in early March 1933, Roosevelt pushed through an Emergency Banking Act that greatly expanded presidential powers over banking, instilling sufficient confidence to get the nation's banking system up and running again. A few months later, the Glass-Steagall Banking Act introduced fundamental banking reform, once again through a combination of regulation and insurance. The act required separation of commercial and investment banking (thereby segregating out the riskier investment activity from more manageable conventional banking). It expanded the regulatory powers of the Federal Reserve Board over member banks. And it created the Federal Deposit Insurance Corporation to insure deposits up to $5,000. The combination of regulation and insurance made it safe for citizens to bank again, and deposits began to grow. The subsequent Banking Act of 1935 further strengthened and reformed the Federal Reserve System.

Equally vital was the Securities Exchange Act of 1934. Designed to remedy the wholesale abuses of the 1920s stock market, the act created a Securities and Exchange Commission to oversee stock sales and granted the Federal Reserve the power to regulate margin selling. Just as regulation made banking safe, so the commission granted a measure of safety to investors and insurance against the worst scams of the 1920s boom.

The Depression led to a rash of mortgage foreclosures; millions of Americans lost their homes, and millions more homeowners were in jeopardy of losing them. In 1933, Roosevelt successfully pushed for the creation of the Home Owners Loan Corporation to provide refinancing for homeowners threatened by foreclosure. The following year saw the establishment of the Federal Housing Administration, to provide federal insurance for home mortgage lenders, an agency that ultimately helped promote widespread home ownership in the United States.

In 1935, Congress passed the Social Security Act, creating the nation's first real social safety net (to use a phrase from a later era): small old-age pensions and unemployment insurance to be administered by the states from federal grants. Both were paid for by new payroll taxes, to which employees and employers contributed.

One major consequence of the Depression was a rehabilitation of organized labor—and the extension of unions from skilled crafts to the nation's major industries. The 1930s were a period of extensive labor unrest, multiple strikes, and violence; however, the pain of unemployment had become so widely shared that public opinion, once hostile to unions, grew more sympathetic. Roosevelt preferred to see cooperative relations between labor and management and disliked strikes. But he acquiesced in legislation sponsored by Senator Robert Wagner of New York to strengthen the bargaining power of unions.[11] Ultimately the New Deal was responsible for two key pieces of legislation that revolutionized the American workplace. The National Labor Relations Act of 1935 created a three-member National Labor Relations Board with the power to protect workers' right to organize, to conduct union elections, and to bargain collectively. As a consequence, by 1940 labor union membership rose to 7.2 million compared to 3.7 million in 1932. The board was also empowered to intervene to stop unfair labor practices. The Fair Labor Standards Act of 1938 established the first mechanism for determining minimum wages, mandated a forty-hour workweek with overtime paid at time-and-a-half, and ended child labor by forbidding the employment of children under sixteen.

Together, these elements—regulation, social insurance, federal underwriting of home ownership, and protection of workers and their right to organize—would eventually help bring forth a fundamentally new kind of industrial economy in the post–World War II era, one in which ordinary industrial workers could aspire to and attain a middle-class standard of living and in which they enjoyed decent wages, relative job security, savings protected from financial mismanagement and malfeasance, the benefits of home ownership, and a measure of security in retirement. It helped put the American Dream within reach once again of the prudent laborer who started from the low rungs of the economic ladder.

To view the New Deal in retrospect, from the standpoint of its legacy, as we have done here, is perhaps to paint too pretty a picture of the events of the decade. Roosevelt's approach was anything but systematic. His initial effort at recovery, embodied in the National Industrial Recovery Act of 1933, was an ambitious attempt to regulate economic life in a substantial way, moving in the direction of a centrally planned economy. The efforts of the National Recovery Administration were not too far along before the act was declared unconstitutional by the Supreme Court in 1935. Similarly, the president's efforts to "pack" the Court by expanding its membership in 1937 were thought to be an assault on the Constitution: it was turned back by conservative Democrats in the Senate. There was a lot of trial and a lot of error in Roosevelt's approach. But perhaps only a leader as bold as Roosevelt could have redrafted America's social contract from the ground up. That the majority of the public felt a need for such radical reforms is evidenced by the fact that Roosevelt easily won reelection to three more terms.

The most important New Deal initiatives have become an integral part of our own economic life. They have become so much a piece of the fabric of American economic activity that we not only take them for granted: we fail to appreciate how critical they have been in reducing the risk inherent in a

modern economy, in effect, making the world safe for capitalism, and making capitalism safe for the ordinary worker and
consumer. Those who wish to turn the clock back to a time before the New Deal often forget that the same forces that produced the prosperity of the Roaring Twenties also brought the
catastrophe of 1929. Economic policies that maximize business
and consumer risk taking may for a time encourage high rates
of growth; but they also incur a much greater chance of economic disaster. The two go hand in hand.

Codifying the Dream

It was the World War II economy that finally ended the long
Depression. Perhaps only war could have justified the truly massive expansion of government investment and government employment that was necessary to sufficiently expand aggregate
demand. From 1941 to 1943, federal outlays as a percentage of
GNP nearly quadrupled, from 11 percent to 41 percent, while
the federal deficit expanded nearly sevenfold, from 4 percent
to nearly 29 percent of GNP. As the ranks of the armed services
rapidly swelled from prewar levels of well under a million to
some nine million personnel in 1943, unemployment quickly
fell—from nearly 10 percent in 1940 to 3.1 percent in 1942 and
less than 2 percent in 1943.[12] Eventually there was an acute
labor shortage, which was largely met by millions of women
who newly entered the workforce.

    As war leader, Roosevelt was conscious of his predecessor
Wilson's mistakes and strove not to repeat them. One critical
error of Wilson was to neglect domestic concerns when he
turned his attention to war- and peacemaking. The result was
an abrupt end to the Progressive Era. Roosevelt, by contrast,
tried to codify the gains that had been made in the New Deal

and set forth the terms of the nation's new social contract. In his State of the Union message in 1944, he described a "second Bill of Rights"—essentially a replacement of the laissez-faire belief in an inactive government economic policy:

> This Republic had its beginning, and grew to its present strength, under the protection of certain inalienable political rights—among them the right of free speech, free press, free worship, trial by jury, freedom from unreasonable searches and seizures. They were our rights to life and liberty.
>
> As our Nation has grown in size and stature, however—as our industrial economy expanded—these political rights proved inadequate to assure us equality in the pursuit of happiness.
>
> We have come to a clear realization of the fact that true individual freedom cannot exist without economic security and independence. "Necessitous men are not free men." People who are hungry and out of a job are the stuff of which dictatorships are made.
>
> In our day these economic truths have become accepted as self-evident. We have accepted, so to speak, a second Bill of Rights under which a new basis of security and prosperity can be established for all regardless of station, race, or creed.
>
> Among these are:
>
> The right to a useful and remunerative job in the industries or shops or farms or mines of the Nation;
>
> The right to earn enough to provide adequate food and clothing and recreation;

The right of every farmer to raise and sell his
products at a return which will give him and his
family a decent living;

The right of every businessman, large and small,
to trade in an atmosphere of freedom from unfair
competition and domination by monopolies at home
or abroad;

The right of every family to a decent home;

The right to adequate medical care and the
opportunity to achieve and enjoy good health;

The right to adequate protection from the
economic fears of old age, sickness, accident, and
unemployment;

The right to a good education.

All of these rights spell security. And after this
war is won we must be prepared to move forward,
in the implementation of these rights, to new goals
of human happiness and well-being.[13]

One way Roosevelt sought to implement this vision was
by passage of the Servicemen's Readjustment Act of 1944, better
known as the G.I. Bill. The bill provided unemployment compensation, mortgage loan guarantees, and educational stipends
for returning World War II veterans. Returning GIs received
some $2.5 billion in unemployment payments in 1946 and
1947. From 1945 through 1950, the government provided veterans with over $10 billion for college and vocational training.[14]

Not only did spending for veterans (nearly $35 billion
from 1945 through 1950) stimulate the economy.[15] It also created a massive new college-educated middle class, whose skills
would add to the growth and productivity of the economy for
a generation. The federal government had been generous with

veterans following previous wars. But after World War II, the money for veterans came in a form largely shaped by the social vision Roosevelt had set forth in his 1944 State of the Union message. Veterans were given immediate cash to tide them over through unemployment. But they were also given assistance, specifically, with gaining a college education and purchasing a home. Americans were perhaps especially prepared to extend these "rights" of education and home ownership to individuals who had risked their lives in defense of the nation. But the added effect of the G.I. Bill was to use government aid to build an entire new generation of middle-class Americans.

The G.I. Bill also had a ripple effect. It strengthened higher education by generating billions in indirect subsidies (in the form of the veterans' tuition stipends) to the nation's colleges and universities, greatly expanding the American higher education system. The New Dealers had hit upon a marvelously nonbureaucratic way of using federal resources to reshape an entire society. The costs of administering G.I. Bill benefits were relatively minimal. But the program's impact in reshaping society was probably greater—and more effective—than anything that could have been accomplished through central planning or government command-and-control-style bureaucratic regulation.

Not everyone accepted Roosevelt's ambitious new definition of economic rights. But FDR succeeded in forging a new economic consensus that would survive mostly intact under both Democratic and Republican presidents for three and one-half decades. In 1945, congressional sponsors of a proposed Full Employment Act sought to enshrine in law the right to a job and legislate Keynesian economics, requiring the government to engage in "compensatory spending" in times of recession to ensure "full employment." Opponents of the act whittled down its provisions. The right to employment was excised, as was the requirement for compensatory spending. The compromise Employment Act of 1946 established government's responsibility to promote the more ambiguously phrased "maximum employment." The act also required an Annual Economic Report from the president and established a Council of Economic Advisers.[16] To be sure, the law did not guarantee full employment. But it was a powerful symbolic statement of the federal government's new role. Not only was government's right to intervene in the economy established; government's role in the economy was now understood to be a responsibility. Like it or not, employment had now become the barometer by which presidents and their administrations were to be judged. As perhaps the leading measure of presidential performance, employment forged a direct link between the electoral fortunes of the president and his party, on the one hand, and the fate of the ordinary worker, on the other. It stood as a constant reminder that the economy existed to serve the American worker, and not (as had often been believed in previous eras) vice versa.

President Dwight D. Eisenhower was the first Republican president to follow FDR. During his eight years in office from 1953 to 1961, Eisenhower opposed expanding government's role in the economy. He stood staunchly by Republican principles of fiscal conservatism. He had no patience with Keynesian theories and had no intention of tinkering with deficit spending to ensure maximum employment. Despite his fiscal conservatism, however, Eisenhower made no attempt to dismantle the legacy of New Deal programs—Social Security, unemployment insurance, federal support for mortgages, and home ownership under the Federal Housing Authority. The truth is, an attack on the New Deal legacy would have seemed almost unthinkable. In combination with the G.I. Bill, the New Deal legacy was helping to create a solidly middle-class society of hardworking, homeowning workers and consumers, rich with opportunities for education and economic advancement. Under the aegis of national defense, Eisenhower himself expanded government's role, pursuing his own program of internal improvements by pushing for the creation of the Interstate Highway System, established in 1956. After the Soviet Union launched Sputnik, the world's first earth-orbiting satellite, in 1957, Eisenhower acquiesced in a Democratic plan for federal aid to education, signing the National Defense Education Act of 1958. Ostensibly intended to help Americans compete in the space and technology race with the Soviets, the act called for nearly $1 billion in student loans and fellowships, further expanding nonbureaucratic federal support for higher education.[17]

The economy continued to grow healthily in the 1950s. A comparison of the economies of the 1920s and the 1950s is instructive. By the mid-1920s, federal outlays stood at only about 3 percent of GNP. By the mid-1950s, federal spending hovered around 17 to 19 percent of GNP, a legacy partly of cold war defense requirements, partly of the New Deal programs. The government of the 1950s, in other words, was roughly a six times larger presence in the economy than the government of the 1920s. Yet growth rates in the two decades were comparable. From 1921, the year Republicans took the White House, through 1929, GNP grew at an average real rate of 4.5 percent a year. From 1951 through 1959, GNP expanded at an average real rate of 3.6 percent a year. However, if one included the year 1950, an especially good year, the average for the entire 1950s was 4.1 percent. By contrast, in the twelve years during which Republicans controlled the White House and pursued their laissez-faire doctrine (1921 through 1932) the average real annual growth in GNP was actually negative (minus 4 percent a year).[18]

Unemployment in the 1950s stood at about the same level as in the 1920s—an average of 4.6 percent for 1921 through 1929 and of 4.4 percent for 1951 through 1959.[19] In both decades, the economy had its ups and downs. But the difference was the unemployed of the 1950s could count on unemployment insurance and were not threatened with poverty and starvation, as were the unemployed of the earlier decade. From 1920 to 1929, average hourly wages of manufacturing production workers declined in real terms, even while productivity and manufacturing profits increased. From 1950 to 1959, average hourly wages of workers in the same category grew by 21 percent in real terms. The 1950s enjoyed a level of prosperity similar to that of the 1920s, but prosperity was much more widely shared. In 1929, families with the top fifth of incomes took in over half of the national income; by 1959, the share of this group was 44 percent.[20] In the 1950s, thanks largely to the legacy of the New Deal, millions more Americans had access to home ownership, a college education, and decent-paying jobs with good working conditions. The forty-hour workweek was standard. Unions protected millions of workers from arbitrary actions by management. Child labor had been outlawed. Banking and investing were much safer activities. And, with or without conscious Keynesian policies, the large presence of government in the economy served as a kind of buffer against a total collapse of demand such as had been seen beginning in 1929.

The American economy that emerged after World War II—essentially the economy that we live and work in today—differed profoundly from the limited government, laissez-faire system of the pre–New Deal era. The contrast could be seen perhaps most dramatically in the way the economy now responded to recessions. Eisenhower presided over no fewer than three recessions in the course of his eight years in office—in 1953–54, 1957–58, and 1960–61. Yet by comparison to pre–World War II downturns, the Eisenhower recessions were remarkably short and mild.

The three Eisenhower recessions lasted an average of just over nine months each. Unemployment peaked in 1958, at 6.8 percent. By contrast, from 1869 through 1933, economic downturns had typically lasted an average of twenty-three months. From 1869, the dawn of the Gilded Age, through 1933, the U.S. economy suffered seventeen downturns. Of these, three dragged on for more than three years, five persisted for two years or longer, and only one ended in fewer than ten months. Moreover, the earlier slumps had typically brought catastrophic levels of unemployment, typically in the range of 12 to 25 percent.[21]

Something had clearly improved. What had happened? The most obvious answer was that the federal government had significantly grown. It was now an economic force to be reckoned with. During the mid-1920s, federal outlays amounted to only about 3 percent of GNP. By the mid-1950s, federal outlays had risen to 18 percent of GNP. Not all of this was social spending: about 60 percent of the budget was going to defense.[22] Nonetheless, the new expanded government was providing a substantial cushion against economic free fall. As the economy slowed in postwar recessions, federal revenues naturally dropped, but federal expenditures continued at a high level. And now the government was large enough for these expenditures to matter. They substantially stimulated the economy by sustaining aggregate demand with increased federal spending largely because of the New Deal program of unemployment insurance. As unemployment went up, federal disbursements for unemployment payments went up simultaneously. This "automatic" support for aggregate demand kicked in essentially immediately when recessions occurred and employment declined.

The post–World War II federal budget had become, in short, a kind of Keynesian counterdepression machine. It automatically produced additional government spending whenever the economy began descending into a slump. The result was a pronounced moderation of downturns. The fiscal stimulus from increased government expenditures was an important hedge against an economic tailspin.

Moreover, the Keynesian principles now operating in the economy had wide acceptance across the political spectrum. In the wake of the recession of 1953–54, Arthur F. Burns, chairman of Eisenhower's Council of Economic Advisers, openly acknowledged the role of Keynesian demand mechanisms in ensuring a mild and short downturn. "During the last year," he told the Economic Club of Detroit in 1954, "very few students of affairs seriously urged that taxes be increased to wipe out the public deficit; or that interest rates be raised to speed the liquidation of excessive inventories and of superfluous industrial plants; or that banks call in their loans and reduce the outstanding money supply in order to protect their solvency. . . . Yet, incredible as it may seem, these were precisely the remedies for curing a business recession that had had a considerable vogue in earlier times."[23] It was Keynes who had shown why the old prescriptions failed to work and pointed to the new solution based on government action to sustain aggregate demand. At the beginning of the 1953–54 recession, some still worried about a repeat of 1929. The mild recession of 1953–54 marked a historical turning point. It showed that the basic problem behind the Great Depression had probably been solved; the limited government, laissez-faire economy—the philosophy of the Gospel of Wealth—with all its attendant booms and busts and terrible risks, was now a thing of the past.

Keynesianism had thus become the consensus position among both Republicans and Democrats. But a new debate was already emerging between those who believed the economy was doing remarkably well and those who believed it might do even better.

The Neo-Keynesian Economics

Seen from a distance of decades, U.S. economic performance in the Eisenhower years (1953 through 1960) left little to complain about. Despite the three short slumps, GNP grew at a healthy annual real average of 3 percent. Unemployment averaged less than 5 percent, while inflation, averaging less than 1.5 percent, remained minimal. Prosperity was not limited to the richest Americans. Between 1950 and 1960, median family income in the United States rose by more than a third in real terms. The portion of Americans owning their own homes steadily expanded from 55 to 62 percent. As the economy grew, poverty declined by perhaps as much as a third, from roughly 30 percent of the population in 1950 to about 20 percent in 1960.[24]

But the conviction was strong among a new generation of Keynesian economists that they could do better. The peace and prosperity of the 1950s had brought forth a kind of intellectual renaissance in American universities, spurred by the coming of age of the modern social sciences. In an array of fields, from defense thinking, to business management, to social policy and economics, a new generation of university-based social scientists had built up an arsenal of theories, innovative methods, and fresh approaches—which they were now eager to try out in the real world.

Nowhere was the activity more energetic than in the field of modern economics. Keynes's thinking had furnished economists with extraordinarily powerful fiscal tools to manage the economy. But throughout the 1950s American economists attempted to improve on Keynes's work. In the process, they subtly changed its thrust. Under the influence of a number of academic economists, Keynesianism gradually evolved in the 1950s from a broad answer to the crisis of depressions and massive unemployment into a neo-Keynesian tool of social engineering, a method for massaging the modern economy to coax a bit more performance out of it.

The neo-Keynesian economics developed in the 1950s was based on a simple proposition: if deficit spending could lower unemployment in a recession, could it not also be used to reduce unemployment to an even lower level during a boom? That is, might not deficit spending hold the key to permanently reducing unemployment to levels below the 4 to 5 percent range that seemed to persist even when the U.S. economy was doing well? And would not such a reduction in unemployment lead to even stronger growth and greater national income?

A turning point came in 1958, with the publication of an article by the British economist A. W. H. Phillips.[25] The article focused on the historical relationship between unemployment and inflation. Phillips showed how in the United Kingdom these two numbers had historically tended to seesaw. When inflation was low, unemployment rose. When inflation increased, unemployment declined. He pictured the relationship between the unemployment and inflation rates graphically in what famously became known as the Phillips Curve.

Two American Keynesians, Paul A. Samuelson and Robert W. Solow, sought to put Phillips's insight to practical use. If high unemployment went hand in hand with low inflation, and vice versa, might not these values represent policy choices? In the American experience, when inflation was near zero and prices were not rising, it appeared that unemployment tended to hover around 5 percent. What would happen, they asked, if one were to run a modest inflation rate of 3 percent, allowing prices to increase? Would that not, by the logic of Phillips's analysis, cause unemployment to drop to the 3 percent range? In other words, could one perhaps fine-tune the economy, using Keynesian tactics, to produce better unemployment performance than had been seen to date? What harm could there be in a little inflation, if millions more Americans could be put to work? It was a socially laudable agenda, and it sounded plausible enough.[26]

Virtually all mainstream economists, Republican and Democrat, agreed by the mid-1950s that deficit spending was an effective antidote to recessions. What was new in the neo-Keynesian economics was the proposal to use deficit spending during an economic expansion to permanently lower unemployment and increase rates of growth. But the new approach carried a substantial risk: the threat of increasing inflation.

Moving Again

The Democratic nominee John F. Kennedy came to office in 1961 with a promise to "get this country moving again." The question was, moving where? The reforms of the Progressive Era and the New Deal had been driven by a widely shared sense of social crisis. Strong majorities in both eras had felt a need for radical change. Kennedy's narrow victory over Eisenhower's vice president, Richard Nixon, in 1960 signaled no such popular mandate for reform. Kennedy won with only a 0.2 percent majority of the popular vote. The country was in the midst of a mild recession, which had worked to Kennedy's advantage in the election. But there was no widespread sense of crisis.

Still, the memory of the New Deal reforms ran strong among Democrats. After eight years of Eisenhower's rather prosaic presidency, there was a certain nostalgia for the poetry and high drama of the New Deal and Roosevelt's first one hundred days—and a certain almost ritualistic evocation of the New Deal's symbolism. Kennedy would christen his administration's program the New Frontier, and Kennedy aides would speak reverently of the young president's first one hundred days, as though Kennedy's reign promised to equal FDR's in boldness and accomplishments.

But the spirit of the New Frontier was in many respects quite different from that of the New Deal. The byword of the New Frontier was pragmatism. It was not so much that the Kennedy administration set out, in an ideological or moralistic spirit, to solve vast economic problems or right big social wrongs. Rather, it came to office with a confidence that it had superior *technical* solutions to the problems of modern governance. Kennedy himself apparently felt there was little of the New Deal passion left for social reform. The single major addition to the New Deal that was on the table—government-subsidized medical care for the aged, or Medicare—was the only such issue, in Kennedy's opinion, still capable of arousing much public interest. Kennedy did what he could to press for adoption of Medicare, against resistance from Republicans and conservative Democrats in Congress—and the adamant opposition of the American Medical Association. The measure failed. But Medicare was never Kennedy's top priority. Rather, he saw the major economic challenge as one of administration, of technically managing a modern economy.[27]

Kennedy himself, cautious by nature, was initially skeptical of ambitious economic plans. Immediately after the election, he rejected proposals to stimulate the economy through tax cuts and deficit spending. Treasury Secretary C. Douglas Dillon and Federal Reserve Chairman William McChesney Martin opposed deficit spending, as did Kennedy's close White House advisers McGeorge Bundy and Theodore Sorensen.[28] In his State of the Union message in January 1961, the president treated the growing federal deficit as a problem. But by his State of the Union message in January 1962, Kennedy seemed to have embraced much of the Keynesian vision that deficits could be useful. He called on Congress to give the president discretionary authority (subject to what he called "Congressional veto") to lower taxes or accelerate federal spending at the first signs of an economic downturn. This was the well-established Keynesian formula—in times of recession, cut taxes or increase spending or both to expand aggregate demand.

Noting that "we have suffered three recessions in the last 7 years," Kennedy argued that "the time to repair the roof is when the sun is shining." In particular, he repeated a call for an increase in unemployment compensation (increasing unemployment payments would not only further ease the suffering of the unemployed but also enhance the "automatic" Keynesian aggregate demand effect during a downturn).[29]

Yet the ever-cautious Kennedy was still not inclined to embrace dramatic economic programs. As late as February 1962, the president ruled out a tax cut in the face of evidence of "continued prosperity." But when the recovery seemed in jeopardy in the spring of 1962, Kennedy was ready to break new ground. In a commencement address at Yale University in June of 1962, the president dismissed concern about federal deficits as one of many "myths" and "old clichés" that stood in the way of "sophisticated" policy. The nation needed, said the president, "a more sophisticated view than the old and automatic cliché that deficits automatically bring inflation." It was not a "political" issue, according to Kennedy, but a purely "technical" one: "The problems of fiscal and monetary policies in the sixties ... demand subtle challenges for which technical answers, not political answers, must be provided."[30]

The economy was technically in recovery, but unemployment still stood well over 5 percent—hardly an improvement over the Eisenhower years. When disappointing reports on unemployment and GNP growth were followed by a sharp stock market decline on "Black Monday" in late May—the president announced his desire for an "emergency tax cut" to stimulate the economy. A handful of legislators supported him, ranging from the liberal Hubert Humphrey to the conservative Barry Goldwater. But most Republicans as well as the key Democratic committee chairmen in Congress were dead set against the measure. Their reasoning was straightforward: the federal government was already running a deficit, and a tax cut would only make it worse. Most in Congress were far from prepared to support the tax cut, and polls indicated that the public sided with their legislators. Kennedy was forced to withdraw the proposal in August.[31]

At the beginning of 1963 Kennedy came back with the tax cut proposal again, this time putting it at the top of his legislative agenda. New arguments in support of the tax cut were now being made by the economists who filled advisory roles in his administration. Kennedy's economic advisers had hinted at their ambitious neo-Keynesian agenda in their first Economic Report of the President in January 1962. The report departed sharply from Eisenhower administration positions in emphasizing what the *New York Times* called the human dimension of the economy. The text clearly implied that Kennedy's Council of Economic Advisers favored not just maximum employment—in the words of the Employment Act of 1946—but full employ-

ment, achieved by neo-Keynesian means based on the Phillips
Curve theory. That meant unemployment below the roughly 5
percent range that seemed normal for the postwar U.S. economy. The report noted that the economy would gain $10 bil-
lion in output if every individual who wanted a job had one.
So not only would more people be employed, but the economy
would also enjoy faster growth. (At the time, with the economy
having recently emerged from the 1960–61 recession, unemployment still stood at a rather high level of 6 percent.) Kennedy's Council of Economic Advisers, consisting of the neo-
Keynesian economists Walter Heller, James Tobin, and Kermit
Gordon, was clearly poised to use deficit spending not just to
fight recession, but to improve the economy, to coax it toward
lower-than-historical unemployment and faster-than-historical
growth. "Heller's Concepts Now Prevail," headlined a story in
the *Washington Post* in February 1963.[32]

Kennedy's assassination in Dallas, Texas, on November
22, 1963, shocked the nation as perhaps no event since the
Japanese attack on Pearl Harbor. It marked a social watershed
between 1950s-style normalcy and the coming counterculture
of the 1960s. But it also made possible what Kennedy would
have been unlikely to accomplish while alive: adoption of his
domestic legislative program, including his tax cut to stimulate
the economy. Kennedy had died a martyr, and amid the shock
and grief following his assassination, he was well on his way to
becoming a national saint. Now, it seemed, almost anything
could be accomplished in Congress in John F. Kennedy's name.

Vice President Lyndon B. Johnson smoothly assumed the
reins of power. His first order of business on the domestic front
was Kennedy's proposed tax cut. Johnson, a powerful former
Senate majority leader and an old hand at ramming laws
through Congress, now basking in Kennedy's sainted aura,

pushed through the tax legislation in record time, a little over three months, signing the $11.5 billion tax cut bill at the end of February 1964.

Yet by the time the tax cut was passed, Kennedy's original motivation for the measure had largely disappeared. Kennedy first proposed cutting taxes when the recovery seemed to falter in 1962. There was an original Keynesian rationale for such a "counter-cyclical" measure—to pump demand into the economy when it seemed to be flagging. Yet throughout 1963, the economy enjoyed strong, sustained growth, with GNP expanding by 4.4 percent in real terms. To cut taxes and expand deficits in a time of downturn was one thing. To cut taxes and expand deficits when the economy was growing at a faster-than-historical rate was quite another. The continuing justification was the disappointing numbers in the unemployment reports. When Johnson signed the tax cut bill, unemployment still stood at 5.6 percent. But now there was a new justification. The tax cut was no longer about using Keynesian methods to counter a recession; it was the new neo-Keynesian economics in action: using deficits to supercharge the economy and squeeze out better-than-historical-rates of unemployment and growth.

Initially, the measure seemed to work like a charm. It was as though someone had floored the accelerator of a new Corvette. As tax cut money poured into the economy and federal borrowing doubled and doubled again as a percent of GNP, real GNP growth shot up to 5.8 percent in 1964 and to 6.4 percent in both 1965 and 1966. Unemployment plummeted, from 5.7 percent in 1963, to 5.2 percent in 1964, to 4.5 percent in 1965, to as low as 3.8 percent in 1966.[33]

It was an astonishing result. The president's Council of Economic Advisers seemed prepared to announce the permanent demise of the business cycle in the president's Economic

Report at the beginning of 1966: "The past five years have demonstrated that the economy can operate free of recurrent recession. Now the United States is entering a period that will test whether sustained full utilization of our human and physical resources is possible without the injustice, dislocation, and decline in competitive position that accompany inflation." The implication was that the new version of Keynesian economics had permanently overcome the problem of recession. So impressive was the economic miracle that *Time* magazine featured none other than John Maynard Keynes on the cover of its final issue of 1965, its lead story devoted to the New Economics miracle.[34]

The passage of the Kennedy–Johnson tax cut occurred at a critical time from the standpoint of Johnson's emerging legislative agenda. After his landslide victory over the Republican Barry Goldwater in 1964, Johnson announced his Great Society program and promptly pushed a panoply of new social legislation through Congress, with costs in the mounting billions: the Economic Opportunity Act to wage the War on Poverty; the Appalachian Regional Development Act to fight poverty in Appalachia; new federal spending for education; and the Medicare Act, which would begin costing the government new billions in 1967. It was a legislative tour de force. The Great Society program was the greatest expansion of government programs since the New Deal. Johnson's startling array of legislative victories stood in sharp contrast to the thin list of his predecessor's legislative accomplishments. Johnson had out-Kennedyed Kennedy. He had almost out-Roosevelted Roosevelt. But it was also a strange way to follow up a major tax cut. Having just slashed revenues, the president was now substantially expanding outlays.

Simultaneously, on the advice of his foreign policy and

defense advisers, the president was sharply escalating American fighting in the war on Vietnam. The air force commenced bombing of North Vietnam in 1966, and U.S. troops were shipped off by the tens of thousands to the war. By the end of the year, there were 180,000 American troops in South Vietnam.

Between 1965 and 1966, social spending jumped by $6.7 billion, while defense spending shot up by $7.5 billion. In all, federal outlays increased by 15 percent. The deficit expanded from $1.4 billion to $3.7 billion, more than doubling as a percent of GNP. This addition to demand was more than an economy growing at the pace of 6.4 percent could digest without an increase in inflation.[35]

The neo-Keynesian economists understood that inflation posed a test of their effort to provide an additional spur to employment and growth. Herbert Stein, subsequently chairman of President Nixon's Council of Economic Advisers, later described the dilemma in which the advocates of the new economics now found themselves:

> In the years 1965 to 1968 a basic question about the New Economics of Kennedy-Johnson was to be tested. That economics called for vigorous, positive fiscal and monetary action to push the economy up to full employment whenever it tended to fall below the target. But the New Economics prescription had another half also. That was restrictive action when the economy rose into the inflationary zone. The first half of the prescription had been followed up until 1965. That was the easy part; that is, both the policy measures and the results were pleasant. The test would be whether the government would

have the determination to follow the second half of
the prescription when the time came for that. In
1965 to 1968, the government failed that test.[36]

In fact, Johnson was adamantly opposed to raising taxes, on
purely political grounds. Raising taxes at almost any time was
unpopular and carried risk for a president. That was in a sense
Stein's point. Expansionist policies are easy; restrictive policies
inevitably bring pain. No politician wants to pay the price for
inflicting pain on the electorate. But Johnson also had a more
specific motivation. He feared that if he called for a tax increase, Congress would force him to abandon his Great Society programs as long as the Vietnam War continued. The war
in Vietnam, in Johnson's mind, was a necessary evil. It was the
Great Society that represented his claim to presidential greatness. Johnson felt his entire legacy to be at risk. Congress,
dominated by southern Democrats, was far more conservative
than its legislative behavior in 1965 might have indicated.
Johnson had won approval for the Great Society on the basis
of a kind of national reverence for the memory of John F.
Kennedy and his landslide victory in the presidential election
of 1964. By 1966 all that had faded.

There was another effective way for Johnson to try to
counter inflation—and that was to tighten the money supply.
Watching the inflation numbers creep up, the Federal Reserve
raised the discount rate at the end of 1965. Had the Fed continued to tighten rates aggressively throughout 1966 and 1967,
it might have succeeded in stemming the inflationary tide. But
Johnson would not permit this. Once again restrictive policies
carried pain and risked slowing the economy and increasing
unemployment. Johnson invited Fed Chairman Martin to his

Texas ranch in early 1966 and prevailed on him to hold the line on interest rates.[37] The discount rate remained steady at 4.5 percent throughout 1966.

By the spring of 1966, the *New York Times* was reporting a division within the new economists' camp. Heller, now out of office, was calling for a tax increase to curb inflation, seconded by Samuelson and other major neo-Keynesian thinkers. By contrast, Gardner Ackley, Lyndon Johnson's chairman of the Council of Economic Advisers, was defending the Johnson administration line that no tax increase was needed.[38]

The economy slowed in 1967, with real GNP growth of just 2.5 percent. In three years, the economy's post–tax cut ride was over. Johnson finally proposed a tax increase in 1968, and the Fed began hiking interest rates in the same year. But it was too late. Inflation rose to 4.7 percent in 1968 and continued to climb to 6.2 percent in 1969, despite an unprecedented Federal Reserve discount rate as high as 6 percent.

The inflation genie was out of the bottle, and no one would succeed in putting it back in for the next eleven years. Part of the problem was that at any given point, the political cost of trying to end inflation exceeded the political benefit. President Nixon inherited Johnson's inflated economy in 1969. As a Republican and Eisenhower's former vice president, he might have been expected to return to the policies of fiscal and monetary discipline that had served Ike so well. But part of the problem was that Nixon hated the idea of restrictive monetary policy. He blamed the Federal Reserve's 1959 hike in interest rates—and the subsequent recession—for his defeat at Kennedy's hands in 1960, and Nixon was not one to let grudges slide.[39] In the end he turned to the very un-Republican expedient of government-imposed wage and price controls—imposed in 1971. These worked—temporarily. In 1971, inflation dropped from

5.6 to 3.4 percent, where it essentially remained for two years. But pressure to lift the controls regime mounted, and controls were gradually lifted in 1973. Inflation shot up even higher than before, to near 9 percent. The following year, as Nixon was forced to resign over Watergate and Gerald Ford assumed the presidency, inflation topped 12 percent, this time aggravated by an oil boycott imposed by the Organization of Petroleum Exporting Countries in retaliation for U.S. support of Israel in the Yom Kippur war of 1973. The 1970s brought the first signs of what came to be called stagflation, that is, high inflation combined with high unemployment. Not only was the Phillips Curve clearly dead. By 1975, with the unemployment rate at 8.5 percent, the country was beginning to see unemployment levels reminiscent of the pre–New Deal years.[40]

Nixon, at least, had acknowledged inflation as a major problem. When President Jimmy Carter assumed office in 1977, he gave inflation a distinctly lower priority. The whole focus of the Carter administration was on reducing unemployment, then at 7.7 percent. Carter believed that the costs of wringing inflation out of the economy were simply too great to make it worth the effort. In 1978, Arthur Okun, former chairman of Johnson's Council of Economic Advisers, calculated that every 1 percent drop in inflation would reduce employment by 3 percent and GNP growth by 9 percent. In 1978, this implied that a return to a 1 percent inflation rate would produce unemployment of 30 percent. Why even try? Instead, the Carter administration pursued an expansionary fiscal policy and prodded the Fed relentlessly to expand the money supply, first under Chairman Arthur F. Burns, then under the Carter appointee G. William Miller. From 1977 to 1979, the money supply (M_1) grew at a faster rate than any time in postwar history. The impact on unemployment was minimal, but inflation predictably went through the roof. In 1979, it crested at 13.3 percent. The University of Chicago economist Robert Barro devised what he called the "misery index" to measure the combined effect of inflation and unemployment (the index simply added the two figures together). In 1979, the misery index stood at 19 percent. The following year it rose to nearly 20, with unemployment back at 7.1 percent.[41] The public was fed up.

"For the public today," wrote the astute social observer Daniel Yankelovich in 1979, "inflation has the kind of dominance that no other issue has had since World War II. The closest contenders are the Cold War fears of the early 1950's and perhaps the last years of the Vietnam War. But inflation exceeds those issues in the breadth of concerns it has aroused among Americans. It would be necessary to go back to the 1930's and the Great Depression to find a peacetime issue that has had the country so concerned and so distraught."[42]

It is difficult to quantify the precise costs of inflation and to separate its psychological effects from the purely economic ones. Even during the inflationary era, the American economy enjoyed respectable growth—an average of 3.1 percent real expansion of GNP from 1967 through 1980. Yet from 1970 onward, unemployment was clearly a great deal higher on average than during the Eisenhower years, at 6.2 percent. Moreover, there were a number of very bad years with unemployment in the 7 percent to nearly 9 percent range. In general, inflation introduced enormous unpredictability and stress into economic life. Year to year, one never knew what inflation rate to expect. In a single year, it was possible that inflation could reduce the real value of one's savings by 10 percent. No matter how big a raise one received, it might be eaten up by higher prices. Mortgage rates were in the double digits. A mortgage could become dangerously burdensome if inflation were suddenly to decline. With unemployment rising and falling wildly, jobs were clearly less secure.

Perhaps most important, inflation robbed the economy of much of the stability that the New Deal framework had originally introduced—the sense that there was a cushion against wildly high unemployment, that economic realities were relatively predictable, that recessions would end fairly rapidly, and that the government had a measure of control over economic life. Maintaining a middle-class standard of life in a highly inflationary economy—providing for one's family, planning for the future—became a much more stressful proposition. Missing was the essential confidence that prosperity would grow steadily year after year—or that the government could do anything to help guarantee it.

What had gone wrong? In a sense, politicians led by President Johnson had used the neo-Keynesian economics in a way that challenged the New Deal consensus. They had tinkered with a well-oiled national economic machine, trying to make it run faster. In the process, they had run it aground. The economy under President Carter still benefited from many of the key achievements of the New Deal—the unemployed had a safety net, the aged a guarantee against pauperized retirement, consumers and investors had many protections against risk and fraud. But Americans no longer felt economically secure. The danger was that the entire New Deal consensus would now be tarred with the brush of inflation.

Just as Keynes's *General Theory* in 1936 had unlocked the mystery of fiscal policy, so Milton Friedman's and Anna Schwartz's *A Monetary History of the United States* in 1961 revealed the importance of monetary policy in determining an economy's health.[43] Nobel laureate Friedman's work would eventually stand beside that of Keynes as one of the two great pillars of contemporary economic policy making.

Keynes, as we have seen, offered perhaps the first plausible explanation of the Great Depression and the first hints of

a way out. Keynes saw the Depression as a result of the collapse
of aggregate demand and business investment and believed
that government should take up the slack with its own deficit
spending for public works. Friedman and Schwartz offered
a different explanation and a different solution. The Great
Depression, they argued, was primarily a result of monetary
policy—foolishly restrictive policies by the Federal Reserve System that had resulted in thousands of bank failures and a general collapse of the money supply. The central proposition of
Friedman's monetarist school was that deflation and inflation
alike were monetary phenomena stemming from the relationship between the supply of money and GNP. If there was too
little money to accommodate economic activity, the result would
be deflation, a collapse of prices and economic activity as a
whole. On the other hand, if there was an excess of money, the
result would be inflation. (The "velocity" of money, people's
propensity to hold on to currency or to spend it, also played
a role.)

Friedman's work on monetary policy was initially greeted
with great skepticism by an economics profession dominated
by Keynes's focus on the effects of fiscal policy. Yet as inflation
became a growing problem in the late 1960s and the 1970s,
Friedman's monetary approach gained credence.

As a corollary of his analysis, Friedman exposed the fatal
flaw in the Phillips Curve. He showed that high inflation would
not, in and of itself, produce a reduction in unemployment.
Only if actual inflation exceeded the expected rate of inflation
would unemployment drop.[44] This eventually helped to explain the phenomenon of stagflation—the coexistence of high
levels of both inflation and unemployment. By the mid-1970s,
the neo-Keynesian economists' effort to go beyond maximum
employment to full employment had failed. Economic theory

was commonly said to be in crisis. Meanwhile, the monetarists had come up with a plausible and coherent explanation for the central economic problem of the era: stagflation.

The difficulty was that if one accepted Friedman's diagnosis of the inflation disease, the cure was not likely to be pleasant. Under Friedman's model, the only way to squeeze inflation out of the economy was to tighten money. Tight money would cause unemployment to rise, probably to very high levels. One might have to endure high unemployment for as long as two or three years before the inflation monster was finally vanquished. One did not have to be a pure monetarist of the Friedman school to accept that ridding the economy of inflation would require restrictive fiscal or monetary policies or both. The politicians generally recognized the need for restrictive policies to reduce inflation. They simply thought that the human cost in unemployment might be too high.

But by the end of the 1970s, the facts of stagflation were so compelling that even Carter accepted the need for a different kind of program. Monetarism, which had originally been perceived in some economic circles as a challenge to Keynesian economics, had become a possible savior. With urging from the sachems of Wall Street, Carter appointed the monetarist Paul Volcker to be chairman of the Federal Reserve Bank, and Volcker proceeded to use monetarist tools to address the inflation crisis. He tightened the money supply by raising interest rates and in time demonstrated that Friedman's monetarist tools could be as effective in overcoming inflation as Keynesian tools had been in increasing growth.

Chapter VII
The New Gospel of Wealth

The rise of inflation under the Democratic administrations of Johnson and Carter paved the way for the return of Gospel of Wealth thinking, focused on tax reductions, support for business enterprise, and a laissez-faire approach to regulation of business. Whatever else might be said about Ronald Reagan's approach, it is clear he confronted a real economic crisis when he assumed office. The stagflation episode marked the worst economic dislocation since the Great Depression. The crisis provided the context for Reagan's program. Reagan brought a new approach to economic policy. Clearly, inflation had to be gotten under control. There was also strong public sentiment in favor of tax cuts. Inflation-driven "bracket creep" had in effect meant a steady series of "hidden" tax increases for middle-class Americans. But the struggle now had taken on a powerful ideological dimension. The sentiment was strong among many business-people, and even stronger among conservative intellectuals, that the American government, especially under Democratic stewardship, had become "business-unfriendly." "Government is the problem," Reagan said.

A small cadre of conservative intellectuals, publicists, and economists sought nothing less than to overturn the reigning economic consensus at its foundations—and this meant going after the heart of Keynes's legacy. In effect, this neoconservative group orchestrated a revival of nineteenth-century "political economy"—the laissez-faire doctrine of old—but with a new "explosive growth" twist. Keynes's great innovation was to discover the centrality of demand to the business cycle. The neoconservatives returned to antiregulation, laissez-faire doctrines with renewed emphasis on production or supply. Inflation, they argued, was too much money chasing after not enough goods. The problem, they contended, was not simply that government was artificially inflating demand through deficit spending. The problem was that government policy—and especially tax policy—was inhibiting producers, causing inflation by inhibiting supply. High taxes were inhibiting work, savings, and investment—especially the last. High taxes were discouraging businesspeople from engaging in business. Thus was born supply-side economics. Supply-siders donned the mantle of Jean-Baptiste Say, the classical economist with whom Keynes had most clearly taken issue. With Say, the supply-siders argued that "it is the aim of good government to stimulate production, and of bad government to encourage consumption." "In many respects, supply-side economics is nothing more than classical economics rediscovered," wrote the leading supply-sider, Bruce Bartlett, later a senior policy analyst in the Reagan White House.[1] But the supply-siders added a note that would have puzzled their eighteenth- and nineteenth-century predecessors. The supply-siders argued that the inhibitions on investment and productive economic activity were so great that eliminating them would cause an explosion of new business activity so dramatic that the tax cut would virtually pay for itself.[2]

One of the major architects of the supply-side doctrine, the neoconservative intellectual Irving Kristol, described the thinking behind the movement thus:

> In response to this crisis in the theory of economic policy, a "new" economics is beginning to emerge.... Its focus is on economic growth, rather than on economic equilibrium or disequilibrium, and it sees such growth arising from a free response (e.g., investment, hard work, etc.) to the economic incentives of a free market.
>
> It does retain the Keynesian macroeconomic apparatus for diagnostic purposes, but its inclination is "conservative" rather than "liberal"—i.e., it believes that only the private sector can bring us sustained economic growth, and that whatever tasks one might wish to assign to the public sector, economic growth cannot be one of them.
>
> This "new" economics is sometimes described, rather cumbersomely, as "supply-side fiscal policy." . . . It arises in opposition to the Keynesian notion that an increase in demand, by itself, will increase supply and therefore accelerate economic growth. The "new" economics asserts that an increase in demand, where the natural incentives to economic growth are stifled, will result simply in inflation. It is only an increase in *productivity*, which converts latent into actual demand by bring-

ing commodities (old and new) to market at prices
people can afford, that generates economic growth.[3]

To a country straining under the excesses of inflation,
such arguments had a very plausible ring. Government was
pumping demand into the economy via deficit spending. At
the same time, it seemed to be interfering with and inhibiting
business activity. It was regulating more. There was the Occu-
pational Health and Safety Administration. There was the Environmental Protection Agency. Business complaints about
government regulation and red tape were legion. Particularly
under President Carter, Democrats appeared to have grown
increasingly deaf to business's concerns. Above all, the federal
government taxes were increasing, as inflation drove taxpayers
into higher and higher tax brackets. According to the supply-
siders, government was increasing demand and simultaneously inhibiting supply, especially via the tax code, which was
eroding the "natural incentives" of people to invest and work.
Cut taxes, argued the supply-siders, remove the disincentives
to economic activity, and supply will rise to meet demand and
then demand will increase to match supply. Inflation will thus
disappear. Supply-siders added to this a special twist. So profound would be the new incentives to "work, save, and invest"
that economic growth would spurt forward, with the result
that new revenues would be generated. The right kind of tax
cut, structured to release these economic energies, would not
even increase the deficit. The specific tax cut they had in mind
was a cut in the marginal personal income tax rate for the
highest-income taxpayers. They claimed that in response to
this cut the investor class would put their newfound money to
work in their own businesses by hiring new workers and buying new equipment. Such a tax cut, argued supply-siders, would

not only reduce the gap between demand and supply but would generate enough new growth to boost government revenues to an amount equal to the cut in taxes. The tax cut would pay for itself.

The supply-side approach was about one-tenth economics and nine-tenths politics. As a political doctrine, it was so cleverly crafted as an answer to the anxieties of the age that even people who knew better began to take it more seriously than they probably should have. To begin with, to call supply-side a school of economics was a stretch. The school had essentially one active and prominent tenured university economist—Arthur Laffer of the University of Southern California (though some of the economic thinking looked back not only to the work of Say but also to the work of Nobel laureate Robert Mundell). The rest of the supply-siders were mostly conservative political journalists, commentators, and politicians—including the editorial writer Jude Wanniski, his colleagues on the *Wall Street Journal* editorial page, Congressman Jack Kemp of New York, and Kristol—all of them noneconomists. In later years, Kristol admitted that his goals in this period were political rather than economic. "The task, as I saw it," he wrote, "was to create a new majority, which evidently would mean a conservative majority, which came to mean, in turn, a Republican majority, *so political effectiveness was the priority, not the accounting deficiencies of government*" (emphasis added).[4]

The supply-side doctrine was, at bottom, an effort to solve a political problem rather than an economic one. The political problem was this: how to craft a credible, politically saleable conservative Republican alternative to the Democrats' Keynesian economic policies. The problem Republican conservatives faced was that the readily available Friedman monetarist prescriptions for curing the inflation problem were tight

money and fiscal austerity, often referred to at the time as "castor oil economics." When the conservative former California
governor Ronald Reagan challenged President Gerald Ford for
the Republican nomination in 1976, Reagan went to the public
with precisely such an economic prescription. Balanced budgets. Fiscal responsibility. Belt tightening. It did not sell very
well. Reagan lost to Ford, and Ford lost to the Democrat Jimmy
Carter.[5]

The political thinking behind the supply-side program
was in fact as sophisticated as its economic thinking was sus-
pect. Kristol, like most of the first-generation neoconservatives, was a former man of the Left. As such, he had few of the
Republican reflexes when it came to such topics as taxation
and "big government." He could perceive the strong sense of
discontent among the electorate under President Carter, which
Kristol shared. Kristol also believed that the government had
become too antibusiness. Yet at the same time, he understood
the classic weaknesses of the standard Republican fiscal restraint message, weaknesses going back to the failed Barry
Goldwater campaign of 1964. They were essentially two. First,
the conservative message was too dour—all castor oil and no
fun. Second, conservatives had a habit of attacking New Deal
programs that remained quite popular among most Americans. For decades, in such venues as *National Review,* American conservatives had been railing against Social Security, pos-
sibly the most popular U.S. government program ever devised.

Supply-side economics was an essential part of Kristol's
deliberate makeover of American conservatism. In executing
this makeover, he cooperated closely with the dynamic young
Congressman Kemp.[6] Both had new ideas for the Republicans.
The first task was to give the Republicans an upbeat, optimistic, saleable economic platform that was probusiness and

populist at the same time. The supply-side tax cut provided
that. The second task was to get the Republicans out of the
business of attacking the New Deal. The key was to draw a
sharp line between the New Deal programs, which were popular, and the Great Society programs, which by and large were
not. It was fine to attack Great Society programs, but key New
Deal programs, especially Social Security, should be treated as
sacrosanct (even one Great Society program, Medicare, was
not to be attacked because it enjoyed widespread public support comparable to that of Social Security). [7]

As for the economics of supply-side doctrine, few economists believed that supply-side tax cuts would pay for themselves. The consensus view among economists was probably
expressed by Alan Greenspan, former chairman of President
Ford's Council of Economic Advisers. He thought the tax cut
might generate 20 percent new revenue, that is, a $100-billion
tax cut would increase tax revenues by $20 billion and cost the
government $80 billion.[8]

That the tax cut would solve the nation's stagflation
problem by increasing supply was another great stretch. Few
economists outside the small supply-side circle probably took
such a proposition seriously. Again, the issue had to do with
the scale of incentives. Supply-siders presumed the scale to be
very large. But where were the numbers to back up such as-
sumptions? If economics as a field had become increasingly
quantitative by the late 1970s, supply-side economics was non-
quantitative to a fault. Reagan's rival for the Republican nomination in 1980, George H. W. Bush, famously described these
supply-side ideas as "voodoo economics."

Yet the thinking of economists mattered less than the
thinking of the new standard-bearer of the conservative Republican movement, Ronald Reagan. Reagan would be by far

the most conservative politician to occupy the Oval Office
since Herbert Hoover. A former union leader and onetime ardent Democrat devoted to the New Deal, Reagan made the
journey from liberalism to conservatism while working as a
spokesman for General Electric in the 1950s. As early as the late
1950s, he was inveighing against the size and intrusiveness of
the federal government—under none other than the Republican president Eisenhower. Reagan's GE stump speech, later expanded into a famous television address on behalf of the Republican candidate Goldwater in 1964, was a distillation of the
1920s Gospel of Wealth creed. He lamented government intrusiveness, lambasted bureaucratic "do-gooders," and routinely
raised questions about Social Security. He campaigned against
adoption of Medicare in the 1960s. He preached self-reliance.
His complaints about the size and power of government
clearly went beyond concerns about the Great Society. As an
apostate Democrat, Reagan found himself increasingly at odds
with the New Deal itself—though he remained an admirer of
FDR and borrowed generously from his rhetoric and style.
After his victory in the election of 1980, President Reagan had
the portrait of Calvin Coolidge brought down from the White
House attic, dusted off, and hung prominently in the Cabinet
Room. The gesture, suggesting a desire to return to the pre–
New Deal world of the 1920s, probably expressed where his
heart lay.[9]

Reagan was also an extraordinarily able and, at sixty-
eight years of age, a very seasoned politician. He had won two
terms as California governor and, while preserving his image
as a tough-talking conservative, had shown a pragmatic willingness to compromise when circumstances required (as governor, he signed a major state tax increase). He had an ability
to learn from his political mistakes. His radical proposals for

cutting the federal government and his seemingly hostile remarks about Social Security had helped cost him the nomination in his presidential run against Ford in 1976. He grasped
instinctively the need to reshape his message. He hated taxes.
And he snapped up the proposal for the supply-side tax cut.
Indeed, the proposal was almost tailor-made for him. He
wished to cut the size of government, and a tax cut would be
an effective first step. He also knew that taxes had become a
cutting-edge populist issue. In 1978, Californians had passed a
ballot initiative, Proposition 13, imposing draconian limits on
state spending, as part of a grassroots "tax revolt." Clearly, resentment of inflation-driven high taxes was percolating up
from an anxious electorate. Finally, an inveterate optimist,
Reagan was just Pollyannaish enough to accept the supply-
siders' claim (shown in a graph apparently sketched for him on
a restaurant napkin by Laffer) that the tax cut would pay for
itself.[10]

Reagan also had a strain of realism that would prove critical to his ability to address the economic problems of the U.S.
economy in the 1980s. He understood early on that wringing
inflation out of the economy would probably require a dose of
castor oil. "I'm afraid this country is going to have to suffer
two, three years of hard times to pay for the binge we've been
on," he said in 1978.[11] He had been in frequent touch with
Friedman over the years and at heart was probably as much a
monetarist as a supply-sider. The majority of his economic advisers would probably be classed as monetarists, but the proposal for the supply-side tax cut became a centerpiece of his
campaign. It was just too politically appealing to pass up.

Reagan's greatest talent as a politician was an ability to
communicate symbolically, to paint his policies in bold strokes
that the public could understand. His economic policies were

perhaps in some ways bold enough. But in the end the impact of his policy choices—particularly his fiscal policy choices—on the shape of the economy and the government was far less profound than his rhetoric might have suggested. In 1980, the year before Reagan assumed office, federal outlays amounted to 22.3 percent of Gross Domestic Product (GDP). By his last year in office, federal outlays stood at 22.1 percent of GDP. This hardly amounted to an epochal change or a major shrinking of the size of government. Taxes showed a bit more of a shift: federal revenues totaled 19.6 percent of GDP in 1980 and fell to 18.9 percent by 1988. But again the small scale of this change belied the grand scale of the Reagan rhetoric. He had hardly rolled back the tax code. Federal revenues as a share of GDP had actually been lower under President Ford.

Yet as much as Reagan talked about changing the politics of the country, he put his real effort into changing the country's mind. He sought to repeal the post–New Deal Keynesian mind-set. He sought to instill the idea that government should not attempt to overmanage the economy, that effective government policy should defer to business interests and economic laws. He sought to replace the idea of government as economic steward and manager with the notion of the free market as king. Low taxes. Less government regulation. Fewer government programs. Economic freedom. Incentives. Economic success based entirely on self-reliance. Such ideas had found little resonance among the majority of Americans from 1950 to 1980. Reagan revived these concepts and, over time, persuaded much of the public that they were sound ideas. More than he reshaped fiscal policy, he changed the terms of the economic debate.

He set forth the philosophical framework in straightforward language in his Inaugural Address: "In this present crisis, government is not the solution to our problem; government is the problem." Already during the 1980 campaign, a debate was under way on the merits of demand-side versus supply-side economics (demand-side became a popular term for Keynesianism, following the adoption of the supply-side label by Kristol et al.). In his economic message to Congress in February 1981, Reagan declared his opposition to the Keynesian approach to fiscal policy: "The taxing power of Government must be used to provide revenues for legitimate Government purposes. It must not be used to regulate the economy or bring about social change." He also announced his support for a restrictive monetary policy, along the lines recommended by Friedman, calling for a "national monetary policy that does not allow money growth to increase faster than the growth of goods and services."[12]

Yet there was a certain amount of legerdemain in Reagan's approach. While the decline in inflation and the return to prosperity were achieved through the monetarist policies of the Fed under Chairman Paul Volcker, Reagan argued that they were caused by his tax cuts. Because the tax cuts had been based on a supply-side philosophy, Reagan and his supporters attributed the return to prosperity to supply-side effects of his tax reduction program.

The real story was more complex and quite different in its implications. First, much of Reagan's 1981 tax cut simply reversed the bracket creep of the previous decade and a half—the involuntary, unlegislated tax increases that resulted from galloping inflation. Reagan's tax cut brought taxes back to where they had stood as a percentage of GDP in 1968—at the height of the Great Society. Second, the Reagan tax cuts had a notably weak effect on both growth and investment. Despite the 1981 tax cuts, GDP in 1982 fell by 1.9 percent in real terms. Business investment (gross nonresidential fixed investment) was negative. Growth of GDP rose by 4.5 percent in 1983, but business investment growth remained negative.

Not until 1984 did the U.S. economy really turn around; GDP jumped by 7.2 percent in real terms, while business investment skyrocketed by 17.7 percent. By then the tax cut was old news. What had changed? By pursuing a steady monetarist agenda and relentlessly tightening the money supply, the Federal Reserve under Chairman Volcker had squeezed inflation out of the U.S. economy. The costs had been high: unemployment in 1982 and 1983 stood at nearly 10 percent and was still at 7.5 percent in 1984 but on its way down. For the first time since the late 1960s, inflation had remained absolutely steady for two straight years. Inflation was still high by historical standards: 3.8 percent in 1982 and 1983, and 3.9 percent in 1984. But it was well below its 13.3 percent peak in 1979, and most important, it was not increasing; it was apparently under control. Two years of lower inflation rejuvenated the economy. The effect on consumer demand and business confidence was palpable. Consumers increased their purchasing, and businesses energetically invested to meet the higher demand of the revived economy.[13]

Reagan had initially promised tax cuts to be followed by major cuts in federal government spending. Predictably, however, the inevitably unpopular spending cuts had proved difficult to follow through on. And Reagan's Cold War priority of building up U.S. military strength against the Soviet Union collided directly with his tax-cutting agenda. Yet remarkably, even with deficits in the range of 4 to 6 percent of GDP—much higher than Johnson's—growing inflation failed to rear its head.

The 1980s were in truth a decisive affirmation of the value of the tools of monetarism. And to the degree that Reagan can be credited for the economic turnaround, the credit

lay mainly in his willingness to ride out a recession in order to
have the Volcker Fed impose the needed monetary discipline.
Yet Reagan continued to attribute the transformation to supply-side tax cuts. Supply-side economics started out in life
more as a political story than a serious economic theory. And
when implemented, it remained so. Indeed, the economic numbers show very little evidence of the promised supply-side
effect. But the political success of Reagan's supply-side rhetoric captured increasing public support.

With the Reagan tax cuts came a new economic and political philosophy, a return in many respects to the nineteenth-
century Gospel of Wealth. Attention shifted from the ordinary
worker to the exceptional entrepreneur, what supply-siders
liked to call, in language almost reminiscent of Social Darwin-
ist days, our "most productive citizens."[14] The key to a healthy
economy was making sure these most productive citizens were
free to be productive; it was they who "created wealth" for the
rest. Government simply needed to get out of the way.

Perhaps the clearest indication of the fundamental shift
in perspective was the gradual refocusing of attention from
employment to overall economic growth (growth in GDP) as
the main barometer of economic health and presidential performance. As long as there was growth, wealth would eventually
also find its way into the hands of, well, the less productive.
Critics disparaged the approach as "trickle-down economics,"
recalling the phrase of Andrew Mellon.

Ironically, however, Reagan's supply-side tax cuts and the
shift to a laissez-faire regulatory philosophy in the end had
little to do with the economic recovery of the 1980s. The key to
a return to economic health lay almost entirely in defeating inflation, and this was a matter not of taxes or spending, but of
monetary policy, controlled not by the president but by the

chairman of the Federal Reserve. Credit for the recovery of the eighties lies mostly in the willingness of Chairman Volcker to put the brakes on the money supply. Previous presidents, including Johnson and Nixon, had pressured the Fed to keep money loose, even at the expense of long-term economic stability. Reagan left the Fed chairman a free hand. Through careful management of the money supply, the Fed was even able to minimize the damaging effects of the unprecedented deficits that emerged when the supply-side promise of self-financing tax cuts largely fizzled and huge new outlays for defense swelled federal spending. The resulting healthy recovery, nonetheless, seemed to many citizens to provide a vindication of Reagan's new economic philosophy, which shifted focus from the middle class and employment to investors and economic growth.

The political success of supply-side thinking during the Reagan years caused academic economists to take supply-side thinking more seriously. By the 1990s Martin Feldstein of Harvard, who had earlier dismissed the Reagan supply-side tax cuts of 1982 as having no effect in reducing inflation or promoting growth, was focusing his research attention on the importance of reductions in taxes to increase investment. Feldstein and his colleagues at Harvard and at the prestigious National Bureau of Economic Research began to produce scholarly articles on the alleged "deadweight effect" of taxation. The point of this theoretical literature was to argue that taxes imposed greater costs on the economy than the benefits received from the revenues collected.[15] The particular focus of these academic supply-siders was on investment, which they believed was the key to increasing the "natural" or underlying rate of economic growth. They claimed there was an inverse relationship between taxation and investment: that is, the less taxation you have, the more investment you get, and consequently the more growth. They were concerned especially with the relationship between investment and "marginal" tax rates, especially the top marginal income tax rate, arguing that reducing top marginal tax rates would substantially increase investment and total economic growth.

When the Democrats next captured the White House, in 1992, President William Jefferson Clinton argued for a middle-ground approach to economic policy. He accepted the centrality of the market and the importance of investment to the growth of the economy, and he stressed the importance of fiscal responsibility—especially deficit reduction. But he also insisted that government had a "limited, but critical" role to play in the economy.[16] His actions departed from the supply-side consensus in important ways that were consistent with the economic and political vision at the heart of the American Dream. Clinton initiated legislation spearheaded by the Family and Medical Leave Act of 1993, which "cleared the path" for women to participate more fully in the economy and recognized the new realities of an economy dominated by two-earner families. He also supported federal spending for education and training to encourage the growth of "human capital." His greatest achievement perhaps was to preside over a period of rapid economic growth after raising the marginal tax rates for the highest-income taxpayers, adding two new brackets of 36 percent and 39.6 percent above the then top marginal rate of 31 percent. The tax reforms eliminated the long-standing deficits, opening the way to accelerated economic growth and the eventual generation of substantial federal surpluses. Such growth, in the wake of Clinton's increase in the top marginal income tax rate, posed a direct challenge to the supply-siders' claim that growth comes from cuts in the top marginal rate. Indeed, the Clinton economy presented new evidence to support the demand-side view that the principal source of economic growth comes from rising middle-class incomes as the basis for a healthy and growing demand for consumer goods by the mass of American consumers.

The explosive growth following the Clinton administration's increase in the top marginal tax rate in 1993 might well have been understood as a refutation of the supply-side claim that low marginal tax rates hold the key to rapid economic growth. But the challenge to supply-side thinking embodied in the economic data of the Clinton years had a short life in political terms. Entering the White House in 2001, President George W. Bush began to see signs that the economy was edging into recession. Using the recession as a convenient rationale, President Bush aggressively propounded his personal economic philosophy and pursued a major restructuring of the tax code based on supply-side ideas.

The Bush administration cited the writings of the supply-side academics to provide what appeared to be an academically respectable justification for a major reorientation of the tax code, away from progressive taxes on income toward regressive taxes on consumption. And President Bush led the political battle to establish the supply-side argument as accepted economic wisdom. Repeatedly he justified his tax cuts with supply-side arguments:

> Most small businesses are sole proprietorships, or limited partnerships, or sub-chapter S corporations, which means that they pay tax at the individual income tax rate. And so, therefore, when you accelerate rate cuts, you're really accelerating capital to be invested by small businesses. And that's what Congress must understand. . . . Capital expenditure

equals jobs, and the more capital accumulation and capital expenditure we can encourage, the more likely it is somebody is going to find work. . . . And so this plan focuses . . . on capital accumulation, capital formation, particularly at the small business sector of the American economy.

And we also drop the top rate, of course, from 39.6 percent to 33 percent. If you pay taxes, you ought to get relief. Everybody who—but everybody benefits, I'm convinced, when the top rate drops because of the effect it will have on the entrepreneurial class in America. . . . And you all can help by explaining clearly to people that reducing the top rate will help with job creation and *capital formation;* and as importantly, will help highlight the American Dream.[17]

Using his supply-side rationale, Bush engineered a cut in marginal income tax rates as well as tax cuts on dividends and capital gains. Even the estate tax—a centerpiece of Progressive Era legislation—was repudiated as a "death tax." By the beginning of Bush's second term, the portion of the tax burden shouldered by the wealthiest households had significantly declined, even as these households absorbed an ever-increasing share of the nation's total yearly income. Yet Bush argued that this was all for the common good. In terms reminiscent of the Gospel of Wealth, the president repeatedly cited the entrepreneur as the true engine of economic growth—the key to a vibrant economy. The goal, he argued, was to free this enterprising individual from the burdens of excessive taxes and government regulation. Indeed, the president seemed to imagine that America—where the vast majority of citizens still la-

bored for wages and salaries—had transformed itself overnight into a nation of independent entrepreneurs and business
owners. He spoke repeatedly of an "ownership society." But in
truth the ownership society was one in which government
policies increasingly favored wealthy business owners and investors over middle-class professionals and wage earners.

The distributional shift effected by the Bush tax cuts was
more profound than it might have seemed at first glance. It
was not simply that the rich received a larger tax cut than the
middle class, though they did. As the population aged, new crises
were looming ahead in Social Security and Medicare. The
Clinton-era federal surpluses might have gone a long way toward meeting the future liabilities of these programs, certainly
of Social Security. But the Bush tax cuts had eliminated these
surpluses and replaced them with sizeable deficits. The government had been drained of resources; taxes as a percentage
of GDP were at their lowest level in a generation. It was only a
matter of time before the other shoe dropped. At the beginning of his second term, Bush announced a crisis in Social Security. Under the Bush program, the wealthiest households
were enjoying a windfall of billions in income and estate tax
cuts, while future middle-class retirees could be subject to the
prospect of substantial reductions in Social Security benefits.
Bush's conservative supporters could hardly have been more
delighted. In 2003, Grover Norquist, probably the most important behind-the-scenes strategist of the antitax program, candidly stated the goal of the movement: to turn back the nation's clock to the period not just before the New Deal, but
before the Progressive Era—to the Gospel of Wealth policies
dominant during the Gilded Age.[18]

Advocates of the Bush approach pointed to the return of
growth in 2004 and 2005 as evidence of the soundness of the

Bush program. But once again, as under Reagan, the return to prosperity was largely engineered by the Fed, which loosened money to the point where the short-term interest rate was actually, at one point, negative in real terms. Not only did this radical easing of money provide a powerful across-the-board stimulus to the economy, but the sharp drop in interest rates—combined with the rapid run-up in housing prices—helped spur an unprecedented onetime surge in home equity borrowing and cash-out refinancing that pumped several hundred billion dollars of new consumer spending into the economy each year. From 2001 through 2004, American homeowners extracted an estimated $1.6 trillion in cash from their homes (after subtracting various fees and charges for loans and refinancing), according to a Federal Reserve study. In 2004 alone, homeowners extracted a net of nearly $600 billion in cash from their homes—a sum more than twice that (an estimated $285 billion) put in the hands of taxpayers as a result of the 2001–03 Bush tax cuts. As in the Reagan era, monetary effects—including, but not limited to, the equity cash-out boom—played a far greater role in the recovery than the tax reductions. A Tax Policy Center study concluded that the stimulative effects of the Bush tax cuts were notably weak, providing little "bang for the buck."[19]

Chapter VIII
The Current Debate: Supply-Side vs. Demand-Side Economics

S ince the 1980s the dispute between demand-side and supply-side economics has dominated the debate over U.S. tax policy.[1] Both sides acknowledge that tax cuts can stimulate the economy during a downturn, but the two sides view the problem, as it were, through opposite ends of the telescope.

Demand-siders emphasize the centrality of aggregate demand in driving economic expansions and contractions. When demand-siders discuss the potential benefits of cutting taxes during a recession, they emphasize the need to put money into the hands of the vast mass of consumers. The point is to increase consumer spending, which in turn will stimulate increased production—resulting in greater employment, investment, and a continuing growth in Gross Domestic Product (GDP). Demand-siders therefore favor tax cuts that are weighted toward the middle and lower ranks of earners, who will naturally tend to spend more of any money they receive from tax reductions.

Supply-siders turn this approach on its head. As their name implies, supply-siders see production, or supply, rather than demand as the main engine of U.S. economic growth. Their emphasis is on increasing business investment: in the supply-siders' view, higher rates of investment will lead to higher rates of growth in GDP. For supply-siders, a key feature of the tax code is its "incentive effects." By changing individual economic incentives, they believe, they can change economic behavior by encouraging more business investment by upper-income taxpayers (the investor class).

Supply-siders speak of lowering marginal tax rates across the board to increase incentives to "work, save, and invest." But the supply-siders' emphasis (and the feature that makes their program controversial) is clearly on lowering the top marginal rate, and the reason is its presumed impact on U.S. economic growth. While supply-siders commonly argue that tax rate cuts will increase incentives for "work effort" or productive economic activity across the board, the controversial aspect of their program is their heavy focus on lowering the top marginal rate, with the avowed purpose of boosting business investment or "capital formation."

The key contention of supply-side economics is that lowering the top marginal income tax rate increases the incentives of business owners to invest in their businesses, which in turn results in increased production, employment, and growth in GDP. The upshot of all this is that supply-siders favor tax cuts weighted toward the highest-income taxpayers.

Importance of Issue to Current Policy Discussion

Supply-side claims have been central to recent policy debate on taxation. The emphasis on reducing the top marginal tax rate to accelerate growth by spurring investment was clear in congressional testimony at the very beginning of the Bush administration by R. Glenn Hubbard, then-chairman of President Bush's Council of Economic Advisers (CEA): "The key to the President's plan is its focus on reducing marginal tax rates. We are now quite familiar with the notion that accumulating physical capital, human capital . . . and new technologies is the heart of sustained economic growth and prosperity. *There is now a large body of evidence* that improving marginal incentives . . . is the key to ensuring these investments in our economic future" (emphasis added).[2]

President Bush set forth essentially the same supply-side rationale for his tax-cutting program. On numerous occasions, he justified cutting the top marginal rate in order to enhance incentives for investment or, in his usual phrase, capital formation. To cite just a few examples:

> But I want Congress to also understand that it's not only important to drop the bottom rate, it's important to drop the top rate as well. By dropping the *top rate,* we encourage growth, *capital formation* and the entrepreneurial spirit.

> When we cut that top rate from 39.6 percent to 33 percent, we're saying a loud and clear message that the entrepreneurial spirit will be reinvigorated as we head into the 21st century. It's a way to pass *capital formation* in the small business sector in America. And it's the right thing to do.

> When we cut individual tax rates, we are stimulating *capital formation* in the small business sector of America. (emphasis added)[3]

The supply-side argument cannot be sustained purely on theoretical grounds. The claim is subject to empirical factual analysis of the historical record to establish its credibility or lack of credibility. Given the centrality of this argument to the debate over fiscal policy, it is worth asking what empirical evidence exists for the supply-side theory that low top marginal income tax rates increase rates of investment, employment, and economic growth.

A review of the literature shows empirical evidence supporting the supply-side claim to be sparse to nonexistent. Surprisingly enough, a pair of studies by the leading supply-side theorist, Martin Feldstein, and Douglas Elmendorf found virtually no net growth benefit from the Reagan supply-side marginal rate cuts of 1981. Feldstein and Elmendorf noted, "The rapid expansion of a nominal GNP [during the Reagan-era expansion of the 1980s] can be explained by monetary policy without any reference to changes in fiscal and tax policy." In addition, Feldstein and Elmendorf explicitly ruled out that supply-side tax incentives were a factor in the recovery: "We also find no support for the proposition that the recovery reflected an increase in the supply of labor induced by the reduction in personal marginal tax rates." The verdict of leading supply-side economists on the first supply-side experiment, in other words, found no empirical evidence to support a direct relationship between marginal tax rate cuts and growth in employment or GDP.[4]

The Key Policy Questions

Does a low top marginal tax rate increase the rate of real GDP growth? The straightforward way to answer this question would be to examine actual rates of real GDP growth in the years with low top marginal tax rates. If low top marginal income tax rates are said to increase growth, then it logically follows that we should see higher rates of real GDP growth in periods when the top marginal income tax rate is low. For policymakers, this would be decisive evidence and arguably the only evidence of practical merit. If low top marginal income tax rates have *not* been associated with high rates of growth in the past, then it hardly seems likely that cuts in the top marginal tax rate will produce high rates of growth in the present or future, and the supply-side case for enacting such cuts cannot be accepted as supported by historical data.

In recent years, the study most commonly cited by supply-side economists in support of the presumed growth effects of their tax-cutting program is by Eric Engen and Jonathan Skinner. For example, in arguing for making the Bush administration tax cuts permanent, Bush CEA member Harvey S. Rosen cited estimates from the Engen and Skinner article as the main support for his claim that continued low marginal income tax rates increase growth. Similarly, in a *Wall Street Journal* op-ed column backing the Bush supply-side tax policy, Hubbard cited Engen and Skinner as main evidence that large tax burdens reduce growth.[5]

A more careful look at the data presented by Engen and Skinner, in fact, reveals little, if any, factual support for the supply-side argument. Engen and Skinner attempted a straightforward approach to the question, examining rates of growth in the six years following the Kennedy–Johnson tax cuts of 1964 (1964–69) and the seven years following the Reagan tax cuts of 1982 (1983–89). Both tax cuts involved across-the-board reductions in marginal income tax rates, including significant cuts in the top marginal rate.

Engen and Skinner focused mainly on the years following the two major tax cuts. According to Engen and Skinner, "The time-series correlation between marginal tax rates and growth rates yields a decidedly mixed picture; some decades were correlated positively and others negatively." Suffice it to say that Engen and Skinner acknowledge "the uncertainty inherent in nearly every parameter used in [their] calculations."

In the end, Engen's and Skinner's evidence for a growth effect from a cut in marginal tax rates is far more speculative, and the predicted growth effect much less robust, than one would imagine from the frequent citation of their study by supporters of the supply-side theory. Certainly, the carefully hedged Engen and Skinner study provides little substantiation for the sweeping generalizations that are prevalent in the supply-side arguments made by politicians for lowering the top marginal tax rate.

Marginal Tax Rates and Investment

The failure of the Engen and Skinner study to provide factual support for the supply-siders' overall claim that cuts in the top marginal personal income tax rate increase investment, hiring, and real GDP brings us back to their theoretical claim. The primary mechanism by which supply-side theorists predict increased GDP growth from cuts in the top marginal income tax rate has to do with investment decisions by entrepreneurs. In 2004, the combined Bush tax cuts put an estimated additional $69 billion in the hands of high-income taxpayers (those with an Adjusted Gross Income of $100,000 or more), compared to the amount these taxpayers would have paid under pre–Bush administration tax law.[6] Supply-siders claim that such changes in the tax laws cause a substantial increase in entrepreneurial investment by these taxpayers. This concept clearly lay behind the statement by President Bush defending cuts in the top marginal rate on grounds they would increase investment by small businesses: "Most small businesses are sole proprietorships, or limited partnerships, or sub-chapter S corporations, which means that they pay tax at the individual income tax rate. And so, therefore, when you accelerate rate cuts, you're really *accelerating capital to be invested* by small businesses." Supply-side theorists base this case on a single empirical study, by Robert Carroll et al., of Internal Revenue Service data on the tax returns of a few thousand taxpayers who filed Schedule Cs (sole proprietorship) in both 1985 and 1988, before and after the Reagan Tax Reform Act of 1986, which enacted a major cut in top marginal income tax rates.[7] For these taxpayers, business gains or losses are directly passed through to the business owner's Adjusted Gross Income and taxed at individual income tax rates. The supply-siders' theoretical argument is that when a reduction in the top marginal individual income tax rate puts more money into the hands of business owners, they use this money to substantially increase investment in their businesses.

Rosen cited the Carroll et al. study (of which he was a coauthor) in arguing that lowering top marginal rates increases investment by entrepreneurs—a major reason he presented for making the Bush tax cuts permanent. Hubbard cited the same study in his testimony before Congress as CEA chairman, urging Congress to approve the first Bush tax cuts.[8]

But the study they cite does not support the supply-siders' conclusions. Carroll and his colleagues analyzed the returns of a small sample of taxpayers who paid personal income taxes on their profits or losses rather than corporate taxes. Between 1985 and 1988, the Tax Reform Act of 1986 reduced the top marginal personal income tax rate from 50 percent to 28 percent. The authors argued that the lower top marginal tax rate increased investment by these taxpayers in their entrepreneurial businesses.

This conclusion requires close scrutiny. First, the inferences drawn by Carroll et al. from their own data seem at best questionable. The analysis focused on a tiny sample of Schedule C filers. Of some 19,255 tax returns examined, only 3,480 taxpayers filed Schedule Cs in both 1985 and 1988 and therefore fit the criteria of the study. Notably, of this small sample of 3,480 the vast majority (80 percent) failed to make an investment in at least one of the two years. Even more striking, in 1988, after the substantial top marginal tax rate cut of 1986, the small percentage of taxpayers in the Carroll et al. sample who made any investment in their businesses did not *increase* overall, but actually *declined*—a critical fact on which the authors fail to comment. In addition, among high-income business owners (those who most directly benefited from the cut in the top marginal rate) the percentage who made investments in their businesses actually *declined* from 45 percent in 1985 to 40 percent in 1988. This hardly adds up to a robust case for the proposition that cuts in the top marginal income tax rate *increase* entrepreneurial business investment.

The Carroll et al. data on hiring yielded broadly similar results. Between 1985 and 1988, the percentage of high-income business owners in their study who had any employees actually declined, from 43 percent in 1985 to 42 percent in 1988.

It is surprising that small business behavior has been a centerpiece of the supply-side case. We should consider what a relatively small pool of taxpayers these high-income "entrepreneurs" represent. According to Internal Revenue Service estimates for 2001, the vast majority of high-income taxpayers who benefited from the 2001–03 cuts in the top marginal rate (roughly 70 percent) owned no small business entity. Even if the data of the Carroll et al. study had supported the conclusions the authors draw about small business investments, cuts in the top marginal income tax rate would be a very blunt and inefficient instrument for encouraging total business investment or employment in the economy as a whole, since the benefit of this personal income tax cut goes mostly to taxpayers who do not own small businesses.

Carroll et al. acknowledge that individual business owners account for a small fraction—about 10 percent—of total business investment in the U.S. economy. This figure suggests that even a substantial increase in investment by individual business owners would have comparatively little impact on overall levels of business investment in the economy. For example, a 10 percent increase in investment by individual business owners, which would represent a substantial increase, would translate into a mere 1 percent increase in total investment in the economy.

Given these realities, we would expect to see little effect on investment or hiring from cuts in the top marginal income tax rate, and this indeed proves to be the case. The more closely one scrutinizes the "*large body of evidence*" that the supply-siders claim supports their key arguments, the more the cited factual evidence for supply-side contentions turns to sand.

Toward a Straightforward Assessment

It is time to return to the straightforward analysis that Engen and Skinner partially attempted and then rejected in the face of what they concluded to be "mixed" results. The straightforward policy claim of supply-side theorists is that a low top marginal income tax rate leads to higher rates of investment, employment, and GDP growth. If this is indeed the case, then the historical record of U.S. economic performance should yield evidence of this pattern.

We can approach this question in a more definitive way than Engen and Skinner by greatly expanding the time-series data under examination. Engen and Skinner focused their analysis primarily on two small sets of time-series data, the six years following the Kennedy–Johnson tax cuts and the seven years following the Reagan tax cuts (using the two years preceding each episode as a baseline). A more complete data set from the post–World War II period can provide more comprehensive results.

To test the supply-side theory I examined the interrelationship of key economic indicators for the fifty-four years from 1951 to 2004 (see appendix for detailed data).[9] My empirical approach divided the fifty-four years into three equal groupings ranked best performance, middle performance, and worst performance for each of the following variables:

- Real GDP growth
- Real growth in personal consumption expenditures
- Real growth in gross nonresidential fixed investment[10]
- Employment growth
- Unemployment rate

Table 1 summarizes the performance of the U.S. economy in the eighteen years of this fifty-four-year period when the top marginal income tax rate was lowest. It shows the number of these years when the economy had "best," "middle," or "worst" performance levels on (1) real (noninflationary) GDP growth, (2) employment growth, (3) the unemployment rate, and (4) real (noninflationary) growth in business investment (gross nonresidential fixed investment).

The most critical supply-side argument deals with the relationship between low top marginal income tax rates and real growth in GDP. Of the eighteen years in which the top marginal income tax rate was lowest, only two were also in the group of eighteen years with the highest real GDP growth.

Supply-side economists have argued that a low top marginal tax rate would lead to high growth in employment and a low unemployment rate. Yet of the eighteen years in which top marginal tax rates were lowest, only two were also in the group of eighteen years with the highest employment growth. Also, of the eighteen years in which top marginal tax rates were lowest, only five were also in the group of eighteen years with the lowest unemployment rate.

The main mechanism by which a low top marginal income tax rate is said to increase economic growth is by encouraging increased business investment. Yet of the eighteen years in which the top marginal tax rate was lowest, only seven were also in the group of eighteen years with the highest real growth of business investment. Notably, six out of these seven years occurred during the period from 1994 through 1999, immediately after the top marginal income tax rate was *increased* under President Clinton in 1993, from 31.0 percent to 40.8 percent (see appendix).

In any given year, exogenous conditions may have contributed to high or low performance on one or more of the major economic variables. But if the supply-side claims were valid, one would expect to see some reflection of the associa-

Table 1

Economic Performance in the Eighteen Years With the Lowest Top Marginal Income Tax Rate*

	Real GDP Growth	Employment Growth	Lowest Unemployment Rate	Real Investment Growth**
Years With Lowest Top Marginal Income Tax Rates	18	18	18	18
Best Performance	2	2	5	7
Middle Performance	11	9	8	6
Worst Performance	5	7	5	5

*Top marginal tax rate of 41 percent or less.

**Real growth in gross nonresidential fixed investment.

Sources: U.S. Department of Commerce, Bureau of Economic Analysis, National Income and Product Accounts; U.S. Department of Labor, Bureau of Labor Statistics; author's calculations.

tion between low top marginal income tax rates and high performance on the other parameters over a historical sample covering fifty-four years. The data yield no such pattern.

Demand-Side Views of Taxation

What of the merits of the demand-side model? At the core of modern demand-side economics is the argument that a main driver of growth in the American economy is consumer demand. Since consumer spending comprises two-thirds of the American economy, it is obvious that a substantial increase in consumer spending is likely to produce a substantial increase in GDP.

Demand-siders argue that while levels of business investment may vary substantially from year to year, consumption is the principal factor that drives the business cycle. As the late Nobel laureate economist James Tobin wrote, "Economy-wide recessions and booms reflect fluctuations in aggregate demand rather than in the economy's productive capacity." Demand-side policies, therefore, "work by stimulating or discouraging spending on goods and services."[11] A demand-side stimulus to the economy can be applied via either fiscal policy (reducing taxes and/or increasing government spending) or monetary policy (reducing interest rates and increasing the supply of money). In either case, the focus is on producing an increased overall demand for goods and services within the economy.

For demand-siders, the legitimate economic purpose for tax cuts at a time of economic downturn is "to stimulate the economy by putting more money in the pockets of consumers." The latter language comes from a statement signed by one hundred economists, including seven Nobel laureates, critiquing the Bush administration's supply-side tax cut proposals. In characteristic demand-side terms, the statement described the Bush supply-side tax cuts as "too large, too skewed to the wealthy, and [arriving] too late to head off a recession." The demand-side economists' 2001 statement called for a fundamentally different approach: "Instead of an ill-conceived tax cut, the federal government should use this year's surplus to finance a temporary, one-time tax cut or 'dividend.' We should send a sizeable check this summer to every American, providing the immediate help the faltering economy needs. Compared with the President's tax cut proposal, a temporary dividend would be more equitable, more efficient, and *more appropriately targeted at the economic problem.*"[12]

Behind this proposal was the core demand-side view that personal consumption, the major component of aggregate demand, is a main driver not only of GDP growth, but also of growth in business investment and employment. At the core of the demand-side approach is an understanding that risk-averse business managers' investment and hiring behavior respond primarily to increased demand for their products and services. Their principal incentive to produce more is an increase in demand for the product. To attempt to stimulate business investment in the absence of this incentive is, in effect, to "push on a string."

Note that President Bush and his economic team also agreed with the need for a consumer-based economic stimulus in his first term. Part of the announced rationale for the 2001 and 2003 tax cuts was to expand aggregate demand so as to help the economy recover from recession: and indeed tax rates were cut across the board to increase aggregate demand.[13] At the same time, interest rates were cut substantially by the Federal Reserve to provide a monetary stimulus to the economy. The monetary policies of Alan Greenspan, chairman of the Fed, supported consumer demand through low mortgage rates, which enabled up to 80 percent of households to increase their "aggregate demand" by borrowing on the increased value of their homes. Indeed, this demand-side support was undoubtedly the major factor in moderating the recession of 2001–03.

The Bush administration justified cuts in the top marginal rate not on demand-side, but on supply-side grounds, as a means to increase business investment, which would result in increased growth in employment and GDP. Where Bush and the demand-siders differed was on three counts: The demand-siders rejected the supply-side theory that supply creates demand—the notion that, "If you build it, they will come." The demand-siders objected to the substantial cuts in the top marginal rate because they believed these cuts would drain the Treasury of billions in needed revenue in order to give an unneeded windfall tax benefit to the richest taxpayers. The demand-siders objected to the permanence of the tax cuts, which were bound to result in continuing large federal deficits. The demand-siders who signed the 2001 statement believed it was possible to stimulate consumption and aggregate demand via a temporary tax cut for all Americans rather than a permanent structural change in the tax code favoring the wealthiest segment of society.

Empirical Data for the Demand-Side Model

Whereas the data for the fifty-four years between 1951 and 2004 offer no support for the supply-side claim that a low top marginal tax rate is correlated with high growth in investment, employment, and GDP, if we examine the data through the opposite end of the telescope—and analyze economic performance from a demand-side rather than a supply-side perspective—a different pattern emerges. Data from the fifty-four years between 1951 and 2004 provide ample historical evidence for the core assumption of the demand-side model—namely, that *high real growth in consumption is strongly associated with high performance of the most important economic growth variables.*

First, consider real growth in GDP. The relationship between high real growth in personal consumption expenditures and high real growth in GDP is to be expected; indeed it is almost axiomatic. Since consumption amounts to about two-thirds of GDP, increases in consumption and GDP tend to go together. Of the eighteen years in which real growth in personal consumption expenditures were at their highest level, fifteen were also in the group of eighteen years with the highest real GDP growth, as shown in table 2.

Table 2

Economic Performance in the Eighteen Years With the Highest Real Growth in Personal Consumption Expenditures

	Real GDP Growth	Employment Growth	Lowest Unemployment Rate	Real Investment Growth*
Years With Highest Real Growth In Personal Consumption Expenditure	18	18	18	18
Best Performance	15	11	9	12
Middle Performance	3	6	4	5
Worst Performance	0	1	5	1

*Real growth in gross nonresidential fixed investment.

Sources: U.S. Department of Commerce, Bureau of Economic Analysis, National Income and Product Accounts; U.S. Department of Labor, Bureau of Labor Statistics; author's calculations.

Moreover, as table 2 shows, increased real growth in consumption was strongly associated not only with real GDP growth, but also with other positive economic indicators, including employment growth and increased real growth in business investment.

The data show a strong association between growth in personal consumption expenditures and growth in employment. Of the eighteen years in which growth in personal consumption expenditures was at its highest level, eleven were also in the group of eighteen years with the highest employment growth. The data show a similar relationship between high real growth in consumption and a low unemployment rate. Of the eighteen years with the highest growth in personal consumption expenditures, nine were also in the group of eighteen years with the lowest unemployment rate.

Finally, while the fifty-four-year record shows little association between low top marginal income tax rates and high rates of business investment, the data do yield a strong association between high growth in consumption and high growth in business investment. Of the eighteen years in which real growth in personal consumption expenditures was at its highest level, twelve were also in the group of eighteen years with the highest real growth in business investment.

Figure 1 shows the differences between demand-side and supply-side perspectives with respect to the data on the key variables in the analysis.

Demand-Side vs. Supply-Side Tax Cuts in Practice

The data on economic growth in the United States between 1951 and 2004 support the demand-side view that high personal consumption expenditures have a strong relationship to the performance of the economy. By contrast the supply-side view that low top marginal rates are directly related to economic growth is not supported by the data. To see how the two approaches worked out in specific periods, it is of additional value to examine more closely the impact of the three major tax reduction programs enacted during the period: the Kennedy–Johnson demand-side tax cuts of 1964–65, the Reagan supply-side tax cuts of 1982, 1987, and 1988, and the Bush supply-side tax cuts of 2001–03.

The Kennedy–Johnson tax cuts of 1964–65 (proposed by President Kennedy and enacted under President Johnson) were designed on demand-side premises. Supply-side economists have sometimes cited the Kennedy tax cut as a precedent for

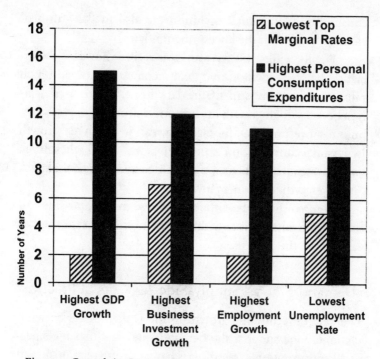

Figure 1. Growth in GDP, Business Investment, and Employment Related to Low Marginal Tax Rates and High Personal Consumption Expenditures. *Sources:* U.S. Department of Commerce, Bureau of Economic Analysis, National Income and Product Accounts; U.S. Department of Labor, Bureau of Labor Statistics; author's calculations (see appendix).

the supply-side program because it included a reduction of the top marginal income tax rate from 87 percent to 70 percent. While the Kennedy tax cut did include a modest reduction in the top marginal rate, the philosophy behind the Kennedy tax cut was clearly demand-side in nature. The Kennedy economic team, comprising leading Keynesian economists of the day, explicitly aimed to expand aggregate demand. That is, they sought to put more money in the hands of consumers, whose spending would then stimulate higher GDP growth and stronger employment. The demand-side nature of the program can be seen in the structure of the tax reduction. The bulk of the Kennedy tax cut went to middle- and lower-income taxpayers. *Nearly 60 percent of the Kennedy tax cut went to taxpayers in the lower 85 percent of the income distribution,* according to contemporary estimates by the U.S. Congress's Joint Committee on Internal Revenue Taxation.[14]

By contrast, the Reagan tax cuts implemented in 1982, 1987, and 1988 and the Bush tax cuts fully implemented in 2003 were largely focused on the supply-side objective of reducing the top marginal rate paid by top-bracket taxpayers. The Reagan and Bush tax cuts put more money in the hands of taxpayers with the highest incomes. According to an analysis by the Congressional Budget Office, *half of Reagan's tax cut in 1982 went to households in the top 17.5 percent of the income distribution; the vast majority of households (82.5 percent) split the other half.* And Reagan's further tax-cutting program in 1987 and 1988 granted substantial additional reductions in the taxes paid by top-bracket taxpayers. The Bush tax cuts were targeted even more directly to the upper end of the income scale. Bush's cuts not only reduced the top marginal tax rate, but also substantially reduced the rates paid on dividends, capital gains, and estate taxes. By 2004, according to the Tax Policy Center, *over half (57.5 percent) of the combined Bush tax cuts went to taxpayers with the top 12.1 percent of incomes; the remainder of the tax cut (42.5 percent) was divided among the lower 87.9 percent of households.*[15]

The data in figure 2 show that the Kennedy demand-side tax cuts in 1964 and 1965 were clearly associated with stronger performance on the major economic variables than were the

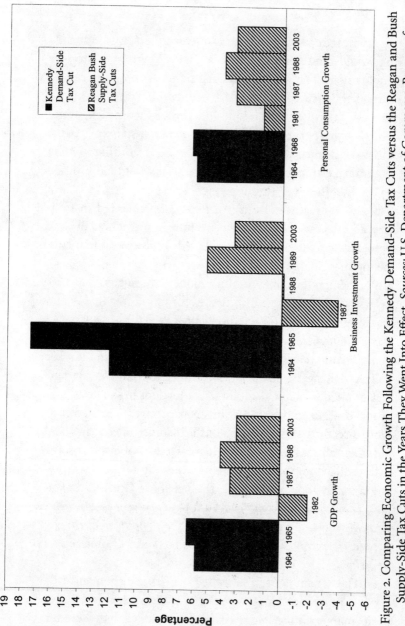

Figure 2. Comparing Economic Growth Following the Kennedy Demand-Side Tax Cuts versus the Reagan and Bush Supply-Side Tax Cuts in the Years They Went Into Effect. *Sources:* U.S. Department of Commerce, Bureau of Economic Analysis, National Income and Product Accounts; U.S. Department of Labor, Bureau of Labor Statistics; author's calculations (see appendix).

supply-side tax cuts under Reagan and Bush in 1982, 1987, 1988, and 2003.

The economic growth immediately following the Kennedy–Johnson demand-side tax cut illustrates what economists sometimes call a virtuous cycle. In 1965, the year the tax cut was fully implemented, personal consumption expenditures grew by a strong 6.3 percent in real terms, and business investment (gross nonresidential fixed investment) grew by a strong 17.4 percent in real terms, accompanied by strong growth in employment. By contrast, there was little evidence of a virtuous cycle in operation in the years of the Reagan and Bush supply-side tax cuts. Growth in the centerpiece of the supply-side program—business investment—was typically in the low to middle range in the years of the supply-side tax cuts. This relatively weak investment growth was accompanied by lackluster growth in GDP and employment.

From a demand-side perspective, a case could be made that the Reagan and Bush tax cuts did not sufficiently increase aggregate demand because they put less than half of the tax cut money into the hands of the middle- and lower-income consumers who were most likely to spend it. Growth in personal consumption was typically in the low to middle range in the year of each Reagan and Bush supply-side cut, while growth in personal consumption expenditures was in the top range in the two years of the Kennedy demand-side tax cuts. Moreover, GDP growth in each Kennedy tax cut year was in the highest range, while GDP growth in the year of each Reagan and Bush cut was invariably in the low to middle range.

What if one assumes that there was a lag in the immediate economic effects of the tax cuts and that the impact was not fully felt until the year following the enactment of the cuts? The data in figure 3 show a similar demand-side versus supply-

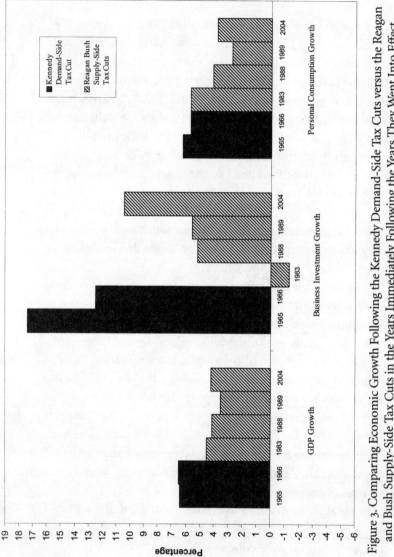

Figure 3. Comparing Economic Growth Following the Kennedy Demand-Side Tax Cuts versus the Reagan and Bush Supply-Side Tax Cuts in the Years Immediately Following the Years They Went Into Effect. *Sources*: U.S. Department of Commerce, Bureau of Economic Analysis, National Income and Product Accounts; U.S. Department of Labor, Bureau of Labor Statistics; author's calculations (see appendix).

side pattern in the follow-on years with regard to GDP growth, consumption growth, and investment growth.[16]

In short, the historical record of the performance of the American economy from 1951 through 2004 provides little to no support for the supply-side economists' claim that cuts in the top marginal income tax rate caused improved performance on the key economic parameters of GDP growth, employment growth, and investment growth. By contrast, substantial support exists for the demand-side view that high personal consumption expenditures (the largest component of aggregate demand) are associated with high growth in GDP, employment, and investment.

Nor do historical data from the American economy support the oft-repeated supply-side claim that the very size of government imposes a drag on economic growth. Supply-siders have argued that virtually every dollar the government takes in has a "dead weight" effect in reducing GDP growth. Cutting the size of government has been a major supply-side goal since the time of President Reagan. Supply-side tax cuts were intended to force government spending cuts. Reagan's budget director David Stockman described the strategy as one of "starving the beast." "The surest way to bust this economy," candidate George W. Bush said in 2000, "is to increase the role and the size of the federal government." In 2001 Bush told reporters he intended his tax cuts to serve as a "fiscal straitjacket" for Congress to reduce the size of government and thereby increase economic growth.[17]

Yet the American economy has actually grown faster in the era of "larger government" than it did in the era of "smaller government." There is little to no empirical support for the supply-side claim that a lower overall tax burden (taxes as a percentage of GDP or GNP) goes hand in hand with higher growth in GDP. An empirical study by William Gale and Samara Potter examined the federal tax burden, top income tax rate, federal spending as a percent of GDP, and average per capita GDP growth rates for long periods in the nineteenth and twentieth centuries. They found no consistent correlation between low taxes and per capita GDP growth. In particular, they note that the period 1870–1912, when there was no income tax, had the same average per capita GDP growth (2.2 percent) as the period 1947–99, when there were substantial income taxes.[18]

Moreover, from 1890 through 1940, when federal outlays averaged just 5 percent of GNP, real GNP growth averaged 3.4 percent per year, while unemployment averaged 8.7 percent per year. From 1941 through 2004, when federal outlays averaged 20 percent of GNP, real GNP growth averaged 3.8 percent annually, while unemployment averaged just 5.4 percent a year. Not only has growth been somewhat greater in the larger government era; the economy has shown more stability in employment than in the years of smaller government.

Nor does the size of government necessarily tell us anything about the kind of role that government may play in the economy. Larger government does not have to be overly intrusive government. To be sure, highly bureaucratic command-and-control-style regulation can inhibit business activity and negatively affect economic growth. But the choice we face is not one between command-and-control government and as little government as possible. History has shown that government has often found nonbureaucratic methods of accomplishing major economic and social objectives. Through programs and policies such as Social Security, unemployment insurance, the GI Bill, and federal tax policies and loan guarantees to promote widespread home ownership, the federal government has managed to accomplish large economic and social objectives with a minimum of bureaucratic interference in the economy. In recent decades, government agencies have found less intrusive, less bureaucratic methods of achieving socially useful objectives. The size of government tells us nothing about the wisdom of government policies. To the degree that larger government chooses smart, nonbureaucratic policies to accomplish society's shared objectives, its role in the economy can be quite constructive.

Summary

The data analyzed in this chapter raise serious questions about the empirical basis for the supply-side theory and particularly about the central—and controversial—supply-side contention that cuts in the top marginal income tax rate bring substantial economic benefits. Supply-side economists and policy advocates have cited a body of empirical literature that provides little, if any, support for their argument. Contrary to the references to empirical data in the public statements of supply-siders, there is little specific evidence in the literature they cite of an association between low top marginal income tax rates per se and high growth in GDP. Indeed, even one of the leading supply-side theorists, Martin Feldstein, concluded that expansion of nominal GDP in the two years following the 1981 Reagan supply-side tax cuts "can be explained by monetary policy without any reference to changes in fiscal and tax policy."

The study cited by supply-siders to support the argument that a reduction in the top rate results in increased overall business investment because of incentive effects on entrepreneurs provides data that contradict such a conclusion. The paper reports that the small number of individual business owners who pay taxes on business income at the personal income tax rate account for only about 10 percent of total business investment. Given these data, the theoretical argument that marginal rate cuts for these taxpayers can substantially increase total business investment falls by the wayside.

Most important, the new empirical analysis of the performance of the U.S. economy over the fifty-four years from 1951 to 2004 presented here finds no association between low top marginal personal income tax rates and high real growth of GDP or investment or employment.[19] By contrast, the analysis finds a substantial association of demand-side increases in real growth in personal consumption expenditures with high growth in GDP, investment, and employment.

The supply-siders' subsidiary claim that there is *substantial evidence for a link between high GDP growth and a lower overall tax burden* (that is, overall taxes as a percentage of GDP) is qualified by numerous caveats in their cited literature and remains highly speculative in nature. (This is the supposed economic rationale for the starve-the-beast strategy of cutting taxes to reduce the size of government.) But as we have seen, historical data on the comparative performance of the U.S. economy in eras of smaller government versus larger government do not support this claim.

Supply-siders sometimes argue that economic growth, though unimpressive following supply-side tax cuts, might have been lower without them. But neither the existing literature nor the historical record provides substantial evidence to support this theory. The central claim of the supply-side school—that low top marginal income tax rates lead to increased investment, employment, and GDP growth—is not supported by the empirical evidence. Given that cuts in the top marginal income tax rate have also increased income inequality—and that supply-side tax cuts have resulted in large federal deficits—history's verdict on supply-side tax policy is likely to be unfavorable.

Chapter IX
The Way Forward

Addressing the Economic Questions

Two opposing ideas compete today as they have through much of our history for the support of all Americans. One is the American Dream, inspired by President Lincoln and carried forward by Presidents Theodore Roosevelt, Woodrow Wilson, Franklin Roosevelt, and Bill Clinton. The other is the Gospel of Wealth, developed in the second half of the nineteenth century and carried forward in the twentieth century by Presidents Harding, Coolidge, and Hoover and more recently by Presidents Ronald Reagan and George W. Bush. The implementation of one or the other of these ideas has had and will have major economic, moral, and political consequences for the future of American democracy.

Early in the twenty-first century, much of the debate between the two ideas has focused on the economic consequences of supply-side economic policies that are central to modern proponents of the Gospel of Wealth versus demand-side economic policies that are central to modern proponents of the American Dream.

The findings of my empirical study, discussed in chapter 8, should put to rest the notion that there is an inherent conflict between economic and tax policies that spur economic growth and policies that contribute to a fair and balanced democratic society. The win–win conclusion is, demand-side economic policies not only increase the ability of all Americans to improve their living standards, but also provide positive support for the economic, moral, and political objectives of American democracy.

Disregarding the evidence that demand-side economic policies provide the best support for our economy, the administration of George W. Bush has taken the strongest steps in more than fifty years to change the direction of economic policy to Gospel of Wealth, supply-side programs. During the Bush administration, there has been a growing acceptance of the idea that it is fair for some Americans to start life with inherited millions, while others begin dirt-poor. Under Bush, America has been evolving into what the economists Robert H. Frank and Philip J. Cook called a "winner-take-all society."[1] The top 20 percent of households are taking in half the income of the entire nation. Salaries of chief executive officers are over five hundred times those of the ordinary production workers in their corporations. Investment bankers and business executives collect tens of millions of dollars in bonuses and severance and retirement packages, while American soldiers who risk their lives to ensure the safety of prosperous and poor alike can barely make ends meet.

George W. Bush's Gospel of Wealth policies have widened the inequality of income between the richest Americans and all other Americans. In 2003, the 5 percent of American households with the highest incomes had a 22 percent larger share of total national income than in 1967, while at the lower end of

Table 3

Distribution of U.S. Household Income, 1967 and 2003

Income Level	1967	2003	Percent Change
Top 5%	17.5	21.4	22
Next 15%	26.3	28.4	8
Next 20%	24.2	23.4	(5)
Lowest 60%	32.0	26.8	(16)

Source: U.S. Census Bureau

the income distribution, 60 percent of American households had a 16 percent smaller share. Under present tax policies, the five to six million households in the top 5 percent income group receive an increasingly larger share of America's national income, while ninety million middle- and lower-income households—representing 80 percent of all households—are finding it increasingly difficult to maintain their standard of living except by borrowing on their homes, their credit cards, and any other means available.

President Bush, meanwhile, has deliberately increased the winners' share of the takings, cutting top marginal income tax rates, reducing taxes on dividends and capital gains, and even undertaking to eliminate the estate tax—a measure self-consciously designed by Progressive Era political leaders to prevent America from degenerating from a democracy of political equals into an aristocracy of wealth.

In contrast to the supply-side winner-take-all tax structure, a progressive tax structure based on demand-side principles would help to sustain virtuous economic cycles in which steadily increasing consumption leads to continuing growth in production and increasing employment income for most Americans, which then sustains increasing growth in GDP. Henry

Ford succinctly summarized the essential understanding of demand-side virtuous economic cycles when he said, "If you don't pay the people enough money, they can't buy the cars."

But there is no simplistic approach to successful economic policy. There is always a substantial risk that either incorrect monetary or misguided fiscal policies can produce negative economic results. The fiscal policies followed by Lyndon Johnson and his successors in the late 1960s and the 1970s produced an economic boom followed by runaway inflation. The restrictive monetary policies of the early 1930s deepened the Great Depression. By contrast, properly managed monetary and fiscal policies can achieve the desired positive goals.

The data for the fifty-four years from 1951 to 2004 analyzed in chapter 8 indicate that demand-side fiscal policies produced the healthy growth of our middle-class economy during the 1950s and early 1960s. And intelligent monetary policies during the 1980s and 1990s were the basis of a healthy, consistent growth of the economy.

In contrast to the positive evidence supporting properly executed monetary policies and demand-side fiscal policies, there is no evidence that supply-side tax cuts for the wealthiest taxpayers during the Reagan and George W. Bush presidencies actually increased investment and growth. Neither empirical research nor the historical experience of supply-side tax cuts provides evidence for this claim. Indeed, the evidence is that very little of the money put in the hands of the wealthiest taxpayers ended up as investment in their businesses or sustained growth in the economy. Moreover, the distributional effects of the Bush tax cuts provided a windfall for the rich while eliminating revenues that are needed, first, to pay the government's bills, second, to begin to address the anticipated problems of Social Security and Medicare for an aging population, and, third, to provide the federal government with the resources needed to deal with new national defense obligations and natural disasters such as Hurricanes Rita and Katrina.

The Future of American Democracy

It is fortunate for the future of American democracy that the data supporting the economic growth case for demand-side economics are strong while there is no significant evidence to support supply-side economic policies. The additional benefit of demand-side economic policy that supports growth in personal consumption for all Americans is its contribution to a fairer and more stable American democratic society.

History teaches us that the future of any democracy depends on a thriving middle class. This is true in both an economic and a political sense. From the standpoint of economics, middle-class consumer spending is the primary engine of economic activity and growth. Sustaining the incomes—and therefore the spending—of the middle class is essential to sustaining the growth of the economy as a whole. It is the key to the virtuous economic cycle. From the standpoint of politics, in a democracy the existence of a large, vibrant middle class is crucial to political stability. The middle class acts as a buffer, softening the age-old struggle between the haves and the have-nots. It is through the middle-class dream that Americans come to share common aspirations—aspirations that help to mute the differences in wealth, culture, race, and ethnicity that might otherwise threaten to tear a democracy apart. To survive, a democracy must also be a community—a society bound by shared values.

From the standpoint of morality the public needs to believe that America operates on the principle of fairness. Ameri-

194 The Way Forward

cans must view their government as pursuing policies that are fair to all citizens, and not hopelessly skewed to those who, by dint of their wealth, can command greatest control over government policy and the distribution of society's resources. If, under the influence of supply-side economic policies, income inequality continues to grow, and America evolves from a middle-class society into an asymmetrical "hourglass economy"—with a few at the top, many at the bottom and ever fewer in the middle—it will be increasingly difficult to sustain the belief that Americans share a common destiny that outweighs the differences that divide us. The belief in fairness will wither, and with it the sense of democratic community.

Conclusion

This book has focused on the contrast between economic policies animated by the American Dream and policies animated by the Gospel of Wealth. What seems clear is that fulfilling the American Dream is a work in progress. Americans need to come together to genuinely meet the economic and noneconomic challenges before us.

In recent times we have witnessed an increasingly sharp break with the policies that forged American greatness and made the twentieth century, in Henry Luce's famous phrase, "the American century." Only a few years ago, the United States was the leader of a powerful and unified Western alliance. Today, as our enemies multiply, we are alienated, in one degree or another, from many of our old friends. Americans have always had some partisan differences, but for decades there was a strong consensus around a society that removed barriers to opportunity, provided a basic social safety net for the poor, and above all ensured that Americans who work hard and play by the rules could maintain a decent middle-class standard of living, ultimately bettering their circumstances and creating new opportunities for their children.

All this is under challenge today. In foreign policy, there is a new commitment to the doctrine of preemptive war. In domestic policy, there is an increasing effort to move toward a winner-take-all model, in which the wealthiest households claim an ever-growing share of national income, while middle-class families struggle to make ends meet.

To build a future based on the American Dream, we need to remind ourselves that the American success story has always been about more than mere individualistic economic striving. America has succeeded because the nation came together at critical moments in our history to support common programs to serve the common good. These programs were informed by core values held in common by most Americans, values which were originally defined by the Declaration of Independence, the Constitution, and the Bill of Rights and have since been elaborated and sustained by our shared history. The values that define the American community include the belief that society should provide its citizens with equality of opportunity, material well-being, and the opportunity for individual self-fulfillment and that American society should operate on the principles of fairness, justice, and compassion. These values include the essential idea that the rights of citizens to the benefits of society must be accompanied by the assumption of responsibility for the good of society. We need to reexamine the premises of both current-day conservatism and current-day liberalism. We need to think through our policy challenges anew and to recover the historical balance between our admirable belief in individualism and our sense of community as a nation.

What kind of a nation are we? what kind of a nation do we seek to become? and what kind of world do we seek to create? Are we a nation always ready to defend ourselves, yet dedicated to principled action in the international realm? Are we still a people, as we once were, committed to economic opportunity for all and compassionate toward the least fortunate among us? or are we a society that now disproportionately rewards the big winners and leaves ordinary citizens to fend for themselves? Are we still the America of the great "American century" or are we being transformed into something quite different—no longer the strong and benevolent nation that once stood as a "shining city on a hill"?

The most disappointing feature of the current era has been the absence of a powerful vision—one that fully recognizes the importance of the American legacy. To date, efforts to design new programs for the future have largely focused on tactics rather than substance. They have been uninformed by a commanding vision—a larger idea of America of the kind that inspired us throughout American history. We must rekindle such a vision of America, if the American democracy we have come to know and love is to survive and prosper in the new century.

Fortunately, the basis for this vision exists in the values that are held in common by most Americans. In a recent book, *Uniting America: Restoring the Vital Center to American Democracy*, Daniel Yankelovich, the leading analyst of American public opinion, shows that the American public has not joined the politicians in their partisan divisiveness. A majority of Americans desire social cohesion and common ground based on pragmatism and compromise, patriotism, community and charity, child-centeredness, acceptance of diversity, and cooperation with other countries. Coupled with these values that promote social cohesion are well-accepted beliefs in hard work and productivity, self-confidence, individualism, and religious beliefs. Yankelovich concludes that the values that unite us far outweigh any that divide us and can provide the basis for a future consistent with the American Dream.

A new commitment to the American Dream is the first step. Wise, consensus-based policy is the second step. *Uniting America* engaged some of our most thoughtful experts to present consensus building solutions to our most important public policy issues. In separate compelling essays, they offer fresh insight into some of the most pressing problems that face us: Daniel Yankelovich on "Overcoming Polarization," Francis Fukuyama on "The War on Terrorism," Alan Wolfe on "Religion as Unifier and Divider," Norton Garfinkle on "Economic Growth and the Values of American Democracy," Tsung-mei Cheng and Uwe Reinhardt on "The Ethics of America's Health Care Debate," Will Marshall on "Social Security and Medicare Reform," Amitai Etzioni on "The Fair Society," and Thomas Mann on "Electoral System Reform," among other contributors. These essays and the independent work of other dedicated public policy experts provide the basis for needed programs to fulfill the American dream.

The stakes are high. In a very few years, our once-revered nation has come to be perceived across the globe, by majorities in nearly every country surveyed, in a negative light. Our nation is now being described as unwilling to engage in alliances unless our allies agree to support our leadership without their input as to strategy or tactics. As a consequence, we are less able than in the past to forge successful alliances to deal with continuing and increasingly difficult issues beyond our shores.

At home, meanwhile, we witness an unremitting challenge to programs crafted over decades that helped to build and sustain the middle-class basis of American society. From the 1930s through the 1960s, American political leaders of both parties shaped policies designed to extend economic opportunity, protect against economic insecurity, and above all to make a middle-class standard of living accessible to most Americans. These policies included a progressive income tax; Social Security; unemployment insurance; federal support for education in the form of the GI Bill, student loans, and vital millions for research; policies to foster widespread home ownership; and programs such as Medicare, Medicaid, and Food Stamps to provide a minimum hedge against sickness and hunger among the least fortunate members of our society. All these measures worked together to create the America we know: a dominantly middle-class society, with great opportunities for economic advancement, a proper measure of compassion for the least fortunate, and a shared American dream.

But now we face a contrasting doctrine that disparages the progressivity of the tax code, desires to change the firm commitment to Social Security, and views health care for the least fortunate among us as something our affluent society cannot afford. New tax cuts have transformed a multibillion-dollar federal surplus into multibillion-dollar deficits. And now the deficit has become a weapon "to starve the beast"— the new parlance for a comprehensive plan to undo the efforts by both parties, over many decades, to use government policies to sustain a fair, prosperous middle-class society. The belief that government has little responsibility to care for common needs, and the claim that government is largely incompetent to accomplish common purposes—such has become a major ideology of our time. Yet such assertions not only fly in the face of decades of historical experience during the great American century: they also disarm and disable us as we face the challenges of the future.

An extremely individualistic vision is precisely the wrong prescription for the foreign and domestic issues that loom before us. In foreign affairs we are confronted by the continuing threat of a major terrorist attack, an unstable Middle East, emerging nuclear capabilities in hostile states such as Iran and North Korea, and a shift in the balance of power toward China—all while our military is strained almost to breaking by existing commitments. Coping with these foreign dangers—and especially the elusive international networks of terrorists—will require a statecraft that understands cooperation and appreciates the vital importance of close alliances. Supporting democracy in the rest of the world requires more than military might to change foreign regimes. And it requires more than building a "city on the hill," to be admired and reproduced by other countries. Exporting democratic values is a worthy endeavor that can succeed only through carefully developed programs implemented by wise government leaders. Above all, these programs should be guided by the principle that success can be achieved only by using realistic means to achieve idealistic goals.

In the domestic arena, we confront depressed wage growth; a widening income divide between the rich and the rest of our citizens; and massive increases in debt at both the federal and household levels. We must also address the daunting challenge of an aging population; large unfunded liabilities for Social Security and especially Medicare; galloping health care cost inflation that threatens to bankrupt the federal and state budgets, making health care increasingly unaffordable for middle-class Americans and a growing burden on corporations. A rethinking of current approaches to domestic policy is clearly in order. We need to overcome the historical forgetfulness that besets contemporary policy debate—the lack of appreciation for the vital role that well-crafted government policies have played in creating the America most of us grew up in. And we need to change the short-term focus of contemporary policy debate. To build a confident American democratic future, short-term, politically expedient policies must be replaced by wise and strategic long-term solutions. Addressing these domestic issues will require cooperative action of the kind that only effective government policy can provide.

One thing is clear: Americans must understand the profoundly different directions in which policies based on the Gospel of Wealth and policies based on the American Dream will take them. Political leaders seeking to serve the common good must reawaken our understanding of the true American Dream and remind us again of what Lincoln meant when he expressed the profound hope that "government of the people, by the people, for the people, shall not perish from the earth."

Appendix
GDP, Consumption, Investment, Employment, Unemployment, and Marginal Tax Rates 1951–2004*

*Years have been divided into three 18-year groups, ranked BEST, MIDDLE, and WORST.

Sources: GDP growth, growth in real personal consumption expenditures, real business investment growth (real growth in gross nonresidential fixed investments): U.S. Department of Commerce, Bureau of Economic Analysis, National Income and Product Accounts. Employment growth and unemployment rate: U.S. Department of Labor, Bureau of Labor Statistics. Top marginal income tax rates: Tax Policy Center.

Year	GDP	% Real GDP Growth	Ranking of % Real GDP Growth	Personal Consumption Expenditures	% Real PCE Growth
1951	339.3	7.7	BEST	208.5	1.6
1952	358.3	3.8	MIDDLE	219.5	3.2
1953	379.4	4.6	BEST	233.1	4.8
1954	380.4	−0.7	WORST	240	2
1955	414.8	7.1	BEST	258.8	7.3
1956	437.5	1.9	WORST	271.7	2.9
1957	461.1	2	WORST	286.9	2.5
1958	467.2	−1	WORST	296.2	0.8
1959	506.6	7.1	BEST	317.6	5.6
1960	526.4	2.5	WORST	331.7	2.8
1961	544.7	2.3	WORST	342.1	2.1
1962	585.6	6.1	BEST	363.3	5
1963	617.7	4.4	MIDDLE	382.7	4.1
1964	663.6	5.8	BEST	411.4	6
1965	719.1	6.4	BEST	443.8	6.3
1966	787.8	6.5	BEST	480.9	5.7
1967	832.6	2.5	WORST	507.8	3
1968	910	4.8	BEST	558	5.7
1969	984.6	3.1	MIDDLE	605.2	3.7
1970	1,038.5	0.2	WORST	648.5	2.3
1971	1,127.1	3.4	MIDDLE	701.9	3.8
1972	1,238.3	5.3	BEST	770.6	6.1
1973	1,382.7	5.8	BEST	852.4	4.9
1974	1,500.0	−0.5	WORST	933.4	−0.8
1975	1,638.3	−0.2	WORST	1,034.4	2.3
1976	1,825.3	5.3	BEST	1,151.9	5.5
1977	2,030.9	4.6	BEST	1,278.6	4.2
1978	2,294.7	5.6	BEST	1,428.5	4.4
1979	2,563.3	3.2	MIDDLE	1,592.2	2.4
1980	2,789.5	−0.2	WORST	1,757.1	−0.3
1981	3,128.4	2.5	WORST	1,941.1	1.4
1982	3,255.0	−1.9	WORST	2,077.3	1.4
1983	3,536.7	4.5	BEST	2,290.6	5.7
1984	3,933.2	7.2	BEST	2,503.3	5.3
1985	4,220.3	4.1	MIDDLE	2,720.3	5.2
1986	4,462.8	3.5	MIDDLE	2,899.7	4.1
1987	4,739.5	3.4	MIDDLE	3,100.2	3.3
1988	5,103.8	4.1	MIDDLE	3,353.6	4.1
1989	5,484.4	3.5	MIDDLE	3,598.5	2.8
1990	5,803.1	1.9	WORST	3,839.9	2
1991	5,995.9	−0.2	WORST	3,986.1	0.2
1992	6,337.7	3.3	MIDDLE	4,235.3	3.3
1993	6,657.4	2.7	MIDDLE	4,477.9	3.3
1994	7,072.2	4	MIDDLE	4,743.3	3.7
1995	7,397.7	2.5	WORST	4,975.8	2.7
1996	7,816.9	3.7	MIDDLE	5,256.8	3.4
1997	8,304.3	4.5	BEST	5,547.4	3.8
1998	8,747.0	4.2	MIDDLE	5,879.5	5
1999	9,268.4	4.5	BEST	6,282.5	5.1
2000	9,817.0	3.7	MIDDLE	6,739.4	4.7
2001	10,128.0	0.8	WORST	7,055.0	2.5
2002	10,487.0	1.9	WORST	7,376.1	3.1
2003	11,004.0	3	MIDDLE	7,760.9	3.3
2004	11,733.5	4.2	MIDDLE	8,229.1	3.8

Year	Ranking of % Real PCE Growth	Gross Non-residential Fixed Investment	% Real GNRFI Growth	Ranking of % Real GNRFI Growth	Total Nonfarm Employment
1951	WORST	31.8	4.6	MIDDLE	47,930
1952	MIDDLE	31.9	−1.9	WORST	48,909
1953	BEST	35.1	9	BEST	50,310
1954	WORST	34.7	−2.1	WORST	49,093
1955	BEST	39	11.1	BEST	50,744
1956	MIDDLE	44.5	5.7	MIDDLE	52,473
1957	WORST	47.5	1.5	MIDDLE	52,959
1958	WORST	42.5	−11	WORST	51,426
1959	BEST	46.5	8	MIDDLE	53,374
1960	WORST	49.4	5.7	MIDDLE	54,296
1961	WORST	48.8	−0.6	WORST	54,105
1962	BEST	53.1	8.7	MIDDLE	55,659
1963	MIDDLE	56	5.6	MIDDLE	56,764
1964	BEST	63	11.9	BEST	58,391
1965	BEST	74.8	17.4	BEST	60,874
1966	BEST	85.4	12.5	BEST	64,020
1967	MIDDLE	86.4	−1.4	WORST	65,931
1968	BEST	93.4	4.5	MIDDLE	68,023
1969	MIDDLE	104.7	7.6	MIDDLE	70,512
1970	WORST	109	−0.5	WORST	71,006
1971	MIDDLE	114.1	0	WORST	71,335
1972	BEST	128.8	9.2	BEST	73,798
1973	BEST	153.3	14.6	BEST	76,912
1974	WORST	169.5	0.8	WORST	78,389
1975	WORST	173.7	−9.9	WORST	77,069
1976	BEST	192.4	4.9	MIDDLE	79,502
1977	MIDDLE	228.7	11.3	BEST	82,593
1978	BEST	280.6	15	BEST	86,826
1979	WORST	333.9	10.1	BEST	89,932
1980	WORST	362.4	−0.3	WORST	90,528
1981	WORST	420	5.7	MIDDLE	91,289
1982	WORST	426.5	−3.8	WORST	89,677
1983	BEST	417.2	−1.3	WORST	90,280
1984	BEST	489.6	17.7	BEST	94,530
1985	BEST	526.2	6.6	MIDDLE	97,511
1986	MIDDLE	519.8	−2.9	WORST	99,474
1987	MIDDLE	524.1	−0.1	WORST	102,088
1988	MIDDLE	563.8	5.2	MIDDLE	105,345
1989	WORST	607.7	5.6	MIDDLE	108,014
1990	WORST	622.4	0.5	WORST	109,487
1991	WORST	598.2	−5.4	WORST	108,374
1992	MIDDLE	612.1	3.2	MIDDLE	108,726
1993	MIDDLE	666.6	8.7	MIDDLE	110,844
1994	MIDDLE	731.4	9.2	BEST	114,291
1995	WORST	810	10.5	BEST	117,298
1996	MIDDLE	875.4	9.3	BEST	119,708
1997	MIDDLE	968.7	12.1	BEST	122,776
1998	BEST	1,052.6	11.1	BEST	125,930
1999	BEST	1,133.9	9.2	BEST	128,993
2000	BEST	1,232.1	8.7	MIDDLE	131,785
2001	WORST	1,176.8	−4.2	WORST	131,826
2002	MIDDLE	1,063.9	−8.9	WORST	130,341
2003	MIDDLE	1,094.7	3.3	MIDDLE	129,931
2004	MIDDLE	1,220.2	10.5	BEST	131,481

Year	% Employment Growth	Ranking of % Employment Growth	Unemployment Rate	Ranking of Unemployment Rate	Marginal Tax Rate	Ranking of Marginal Tax Rate
1951	5.84	BEST	3.3	BEST	87.20%	HIGHEST
1952	2.04	MIDDLE	3	BEST	88.00%	HIGHEST
1953	2.86	MIDDLE	2.9	BEST	88.00%	HIGHEST
1954	−2.42	WORST	5.5	MIDDLE	87.00%	HIGHEST
1955	3.36	BEST	4.4	BEST	87.00%	HIGHEST
1956	3.41	BEST	4.1	BEST	87.00%	HIGHEST
1957	0.93	WORST	4.3	BEST	87.00%	HIGHEST
1958	−2.89	WORST	6.8	WORST	87.00%	HIGHEST
1959	3.79	BEST	5.5	MIDDLE	87.00%	HIGHEST
1960	1.73	MIDDLE	5.5	MIDDLE	87.00%	HIGHEST
1961	−0.35	WORST	6.7	WORST	87.00%	HIGHEST
1962	2.87	MIDDLE	5.5	MIDDLE	87.00%	HIGHEST
1963	1.99	MIDDLE	5.7	MIDDLE	87.00%	HIGHEST
1964	2.87	MIDDLE	5.2	MIDDLE	77.00%	HIGHEST
1965	4.25	BEST	4.5	BEST	70.00%	HIGHEST
1966	5.17	BEST	3.8	BEST	70.00%	MIDDLE
1967	2.99	MIDDLE	3.8	BEST	70.00%	MIDDLE
1968	3.17	BEST	3.6	BEST	75.30%	HIGHEST
1969	3.66	BEST	3.5	BEST	77.00%	HIGHEST
1970	0.7	WORST	4.9	BEST	71.80%	HIGHEST
1971	0.46	WORST	5.9	MIDDLE	70.00%	MIDDLE
1972	3.45	BEST	5.6	MIDDLE	70.00%	MIDDLE
1973	4.22	BEST	4.9	BEST	70.00%	MIDDLE
1974	1.92	MIDDLE	5.6	MIDDLE	70.00%	MIDDLE
1975	−1.68	WORST	8.5	WORST	70.00%	MIDDLE
1976	3.16	BEST	7.7	WORST	70.00%	MIDDLE
1977	3.89	BEST	7.1	WORST	70.00%	MIDDLE
1978	5.13	BEST	6.1	WORST	70.00%	MIDDLE
1979	3.58	BEST	5.8	MIDDLE	70.00%	MIDDLE
1980	0.66	WORST	7.1	WORST	70.00%	MIDDLE
1981	0.84	WORST	7.6	WORST	70.00%	MIDDLE
1982	−1.77	WORST	9.7	WORST	50.00%	MIDDLE
1983	0.67	WORST	9.6	WORST	50.00%	MIDDLE
1984	4.71	BEST	7.5	WORST	50.00%	MIDDLE
1985	3.15	BEST	7.2	WORST	50.00%	MIDDLE
1986	2.01	MIDDLE	7	WORST	50.00%	MIDDLE
1987	2.63	MIDDLE	6.2	WORST	38.50%	LOWEST
1988	3.19	BEST	5.5	MIDDLE	28.00%	LOWEST
1989	2.53	MIDDLE	5.3	MIDDLE	28.00%	LOWEST
1990	1.36	WORST	5.6	MIDDLE	31.00%	LOWEST
1991	−1.02	WORST	6.8	WORST	31.00%	LOWEST
1992	0.32	WORST	7.5	WORST	31.00%	LOWEST
1993	1.95	MIDDLE	6.9	WORST	40.80%	LOWEST
1994	3.11	BEST	6.1	WORST	40.80%	LOWEST
1995	2.63	MIDDLE	5.6	MIDDLE	40.80%	LOWEST
1996	2.05	MIDDLE	5.4	MIDDLE	40.80%	LOWEST
1997	2.56	MIDDLE	4.9	BEST	40.80%	LOWEST
1998	2.57	MIDDLE	4.5	BEST	40.80%	LOWEST
1999	2.43	MIDDLE	4.2	BEST	40.80%	LOWEST
2000	2.16	MIDDLE	4	BEST	40.80%	LOWEST
2001	0.03	WORST	4.7	BEST	40.30%	LOWEST
2002	−1.13	WORST	5.8	MIDDLE	39.80%	LOWEST
2003	−0.31	WORST	6	MIDDLE	36.10%	LOWEST
2004	1.19	WORST	5.5	MIDDLE	36.10%	LOWEST

Notes

Introduction

1. U.S. Department of Commerce, Bureau of Economic Analysis, National Income and Product Accounts (data available at www.bea.doc.gov); U.S. Department of Labor, Bureau of Labor Statistics (data available at www.bls.gov); White House, Office of Management and Budget, *Historical Tables: Budget of the United States: Fiscal Year 2006* (Washington, D.C.: GPO, 2005), 21–22.

2. Tax Policy Center, "EGTRRA, JCWA, and JGTRRA: Distribution of Individual Income, Corporate, and Estate Tax Change by Cash Income Class, 2004," Table T04–0051 (available at http://taxpolicycenter.org/TaxModel/tmdb/TMTemplate.cfm?DocID=625&topic2ID=40&topic3ID=57&DocTypeID=1).

3. U.S. Department of Commerce, Bureau of Economic Analysis, National Income and Product Accounts; U.S. Department of Labor, Bureau of Labor Statistics; White House, *Historical Tables,* 22.

4. Tax Policy Center, "Individual Tax Brackets 1979–1980," available at http://www.taxpolicycenter.org/TaxFacts/TFDB/TFTemplate.cfm?Docid=124 and Tax Policy Center, "Individual Tax Brackets 1988," available at http://www.taxpolicycenter.org/TaxFacts/TFDB/TFTemplate.cfm?Docid=132.

5. U.S Department of Commerce, Bureau of Economic Analysis, National Income and Product Accounts.

Chapter 1.
The American Economic Vision

1. Andrew Carnegie, *The Gospel of Wealth* (London: F. C. Hagen, 1889).
2. Franklin D. Roosevelt, "State of the Union Address," January 11, 1944.

3. See, for example, Dana Milbank, "For Bush Tax Plan, a Little Inner Dissent," *Washington Post,* February 16, 2003.

4. Warren Buffett, "Dividend Voodoo," *Washington Post,* May 20, 2003, A19.

5. George W. Bush, "Remarks by the President at Chicago Mercantile Exchange," March 6, 2001.

6. Aristotle, *Politics,* book 4, chapter 11; Richard McKeon, ed., *The Basic Works of Aristotle* (New York: Random House, 1941), 1220–22.

Chapter 2.
The Origins of the American Dream

1. *The Collected Works of Abraham Lincoln,* ed. Roy P. Basler (New Brunswick, N.J., Rutgers University Press, 1953), 4:240.

2. Ibid., 4:168–69, 5:52.

3. Ibid., 4:438.

4. Cited in Gabor Boritt, *Lincoln and the Economics of the American Dream* (Memphis: Memphis State University Press, 1978), 168.

5. Robert Hendrickson, *The Facts on File Encyclopedia of Word and Phrase Origins* (New York: Checkmark, 2000), 22.

6. James Truslow Adams, *The Epic of America* (Boston: Little, Brown, 1932), 404: "But there has been also the *American dream,* that dream of a land in which life should be better and richer and fuller for every man, with opportunity for each according to his ability or achievement. It is a difficult dream for the European upper classes to interpret adequately, and too many of us ourselves have grown weary and mistrustful of it. It is not a dream of motor cars and high wages merely, but a dream of a social order in which each man and each woman shall be able to attain to the fullest stature of which they are innately capable, and be recognized by others for what they are, regardless of the fortuitous circumstances of birth or position." Adams went on to write, "In a modern industrial State, an economic base is essential for all. We point with pride to our 'national income,' but the nation is only an aggregate of individual men and women, and when we turn from the single figure of total income to the incomes of individuals, we find a very marked injustice in its distribution. There is no reason why wealth, which is a social product, should not be more equitably controlled and distributed in the interests of society. . . . If [the American Dream] is to come true, those on top, financially, intellectually, or otherwise, have got to devote themselves

to the 'Great Society,' and those who are below in the scale have got to strive to rise, not merely economically, but culturally. . . . Lincoln was not great because he was born in a log cabin, but because he got out of it—that, because he rose above the poverty, ignorance, lack of ambition, shiftlessness of character, contentment with mean things and low aims which kept so many thousands in the huts where they were born." Ibid., 410–11.

7. Alexis de Tocqueville, *Democracy in America*, trans. Henry Reeve, rev. by Frances Bowen, ed. Phillip Bradley (New York: Vintage, 1945), 1:3.

8. Ibid. 2:165–66.

9. Ibid. 1:53.

10. Ibid. 2:36–37.

11. Ibid. 2:137–38.

12. Ibid. 2:266.

13. Boritt, *Lincoln*, 93.

14. Robert V. Remini, *Henry Clay: Statesman for the Union* (New York: W. W. Norton, 1991), 210–33.

15. Ibid., 59, 225–33.

16. Boritt, *Lincoln*, xxiv, 221.

17. *Collected Works of Abraham Lincoln*, 2:221; Boritt, *Lincoln*, 184.

18. *Collected Works of Abraham Lincoln*, 2:461.

19. Ibid., 2:126.

20. Boritt, *Lincoln*, 113. Interestingly, the reason Lincoln most admired the great African American leader Frederick Douglass was that, like Lincoln himself, Douglass embodied the "self-made" ethic. Douglass had struggled from nowhere to become one of the nation's most eloquent politicians and prominent citizens. Lincoln remarked to an associate that "considering the condition from which Douglass rose, and the position to which he attained, he was . . . one of the most meritorious men in America." Douglass, meanwhile, found in Lincoln "the first great man that I talked with in the United States, who in no single instance reminded me . . . of the difference of color." Boritt, *Lincoln*, 174.

21. Ibid., 197.

Chapter 3.
The Gospel of Wealth

1. U.S. Department of Commerce, Bureau of the Census, *Historical Statistics of the United States: Colonial Times to 1970* (Washington, D.C.: GPO, 1975), 2:728–31, 2:693–94, 2:667, 1:224.

2. Thomas C. Cochran and William Miller, *The Age of Enterprise: A Social History of Industrial America* (New York: Harper Torchbooks, 1961), 143–44, 190–91.

3. *Historical Statistics of the United States,* 1:105–06.

4. Eric Foner, *The Story of American Freedom* (New York: W. W. Norton, 1998), 117.

5. *Historical Statistics of the United States,* 2:1104.

6. Seymour J. Mandelbaum, *Boss Tweed's New York* (New York: J. Wiley, 1965), 86.

7. Louis Gould, *Grand Old Party: A History of the Republicans* (New York: Random House, 2004), 79.

8. Mark Twain and Charles Dudley Warner, *The Gilded Age: A Tale of To-Day* (Hartford: American Publishing Company, 1874).

9. John G. Sproat, *The Best Men: Liberal Reformers in the Gilded Age* (New York: Oxford University Press, 1968), 126.

10. Ibid., 53, 57–58.

11. Ibid., 8.

12. Spencer coined the term in volume 1 of his *Principles of Biology,* published in 1864. Herbert Spencer, *The Principles of Biology* (New York: D. Appleton, 1896), 1:444. On Spencer's influence in America, see Richard Hofstadter, *Social Darwinism in American Thought,* intr. Eric Foner, *Reconstruction* (Boston: Beacon Press, 1992), 31–50.

13. Sproat, *Best Men,* 205; Foner, *Reconstruction,* 489–90.

14. Foner, *The Story of American Freedom,* 120.

15. David Montgomery, "Labor in the Industrial Era," in Richard B. Morris, ed., *A History of the American Worker* (originally published as *The U.S. Department of Labor History of the American Worker)* (Princeton: Princeton University Press, 1983), 96; Melvyn Dubofsky, *Industrialism and the American Worker, 1865–1920* (New York: Thomas Y. Crowell, 1975), 19.

16. Sproat, *Best Men,* 166.

17. Ibid., 210–11.

18. Charles Dickens, *Hard Times* (New York: T. L. McElrath, 1854).

19. Charles Darwin, *The Origin of Species,* intr. Julian Huxley (New York: Mentor, 1958).

20. Herbert Spencer, "Progress: Its Law and Causes," *Westminster Review* 67 (April 1857): 445–47.

21. Hofstadter, *Social Darwinism,* 31–50; Sidney Fine, *Laissez-Faire and the General-Welfare State: A Study of Conflict in American Thought 1865–1901* (Ann Arbor: University of Michigan Press; London: Geoffrey Cumberlege, Oxford University Press, 1956), 320–46.

22. See Darwin, *The Origin of Species*, 87.

23. Herbert Spencer, *The Principles of Sociology* (New York: D. Appleton, 1908), 2:607–08.

24. Herbert Spencer, *Social Statics: The Conditions Essential to Happiness Specified, and the First of Them Developed* (New York: Robert Schalkenbach Foundation, 1954), 288–89.

25. Sproat, *Best Men*, 207.

26. Foner, *Story of American Freedom*, 119–20.

27. Hofstadter, *Social Darwinism*, 51.

28. Ibid., 58, 62.

29. Cited in Fine, *Laissez-Faire and the General-Welfare State*, 3.

30. Sproat, *Best Men*, 166.

31. Robert G. McCloskey, *The American Supreme Court*, 2d ed., rev. Sanford Levinson (Chicago: University of Chicago Press, 1994), 84.

32. Ibid., 102–07; Richard A. Posner, ed., *The Essential Holmes: Selections from the Letters, Speeches, Judicial Opinions, and Other Writings of Oliver Wendell Holmes, Jr.* (Chicago: University of Chicago Press, 1992), 306.

33. Harold C. Livesay, *Andrew Carnegie and the Rise of Big Business*, ed. Oscar Handlin (Boston: Little, Brown, 1975), 187–88.

34. Andrew Carnegie, *The Gospel of Wealth* (Bedford, Mass.: Applewood Books, 1988), 3.

35. Ibid., 4–5.

Chapter 4.
The Age of Reform

1. John L. Thomas, *Alternative America: Henry George, Edward Bellamy, Henry Demarest Lloyd and the Adversary Tradition* (Cambridge, Mass.: Belknap, 1983), 132–45, 258–60; David W. Noble, *The Progressive Mind, 1890–1917* (Chicago: Rand McNally, 1970), 75–80.

2. John G. Sproat, *The Best Men: Liberal Reformers in the Gilded Age* (New York: Oxford University Press, 1968), 154–55; Charles R. Williams, ed., *Diary and Letters of Rutherford Birchard Hayes* (Columbus: Ohio State Archaeological and Historical Society, 1924), 4:261–62.

3. Allen F. Davis, *Spearheads for Reform: The Social Settlements and the Progressive Movement 1890–1914* (New York: Oxford University Press, 1970), 12, 123–27.

4. Kevin Phillips, *William McKinley* (New York: Times Books, 2003), 31–34, 74–83.

210 Notes to Pages 73–87

5. John Steele Gordon, *An Empire of Wealth* (New York: Harper-Collins, 2004), 271.

6. Phillips, *William McKinley*, 76–85, 41–42.

7. Thomas, *Alternative America*, 132–45; Jay Martin, *Harvest of Change: American Literature 1865–1914* (Englewood Cliffs: Prentice-Hall, 1967), 57–83, 41–48, 228–30.

8. Theodore Roosevelt, "State of the Union Message," December 3, 1901.

9. Lewis L. Gould, *The Presidency of Theodore Roosevelt* (Lawrence: University Press of Kansas, 1991), 162.

10. Louis Filler, *The Muckrakers* (University Park: Pennsylvania State University Press, 1976), 53, 60, 90–109, 162–68, 203.

11. Gould, *Presidency of Theodore Roosevelt*, 47–53, 217–19.

12. Gould, *Grand Old Party: A History of the Republicans* (New York: Random House, 2004), 152.

13. Gould, *Presidency of Theodore Roosevelt*, 67–72.

14. Richard Hofstadter, *The Age of Reform* (New York: Vintage, 1955), 239.

15. Gould, *Grand Old Party*, 173.

16. Paolo E. Coletta, *The Presidency of William Howard Taft* (Lawrence: University of Kansas Press, 1973), 56–71, 126–29, 140.

17. Woodrow Wilson, *Congressional Government: A Study in American Politics* (Boston: Houghton, Mifflin, 1885).

18. Arthur S. Link, *Woodrow Wilson and the Progressive Era 1910–1917* (New York: Harper and Brothers, 1954), 8–10.

19. Woodrow Wilson, *The New Freedom: A Call for the Emancipation of the Generous Energies of a People,* intr. William E. Leuchtenburg (Englewood Cliffs: Prentice-Hall, 1961), 60.

20. Ibid., 47.

21. Ibid.

22. Ibid., 106, 25, 62, 26, 62–63.

23. Link, *Woodrow Wilson and the Progressive Era*, 36–43, 193–96; Gould, *Presidency of Theodore Roosevelt*, 162.

24. Ibid., 43–53, 61–75, 226–27.

25. William E. Leuchtenburg, *The Perils of Prosperity 1914–1932*, 2d ed. (Chicago: University of Chicago Press, 1993), 31; U.S. Department of Commerce, Bureau of the Census, *Historical Statistics of the United States: Colonial Times to 1970* (Washington, D.C.: GPO, 1975), 2:1140–41.

26. Ibid., 1:224, 1:211, 1:135; National Bureau of Economic Research, "Business Cycles Expansions and Contractions"; available at http://www.nber.org/cycles.html/.

Chapter 5.
The Business of America Is Business

1. William E. Leuchtenburg, *The Perils of Prosperity 1914–1932*, 2d ed. (Chicago: University of Chicago Press, 1993), 289.

2. U.S. Department of Commerce, Bureau of the Census, *Historical Statistics of the United States: Colonial Times to 1970* (Washington, D.C.: GPO, 1975), 1:224, 2:716, 2:710, 2:827, 2:783; Frederick Lewis Allen, *Only Yesterday* (New York: Perennial Classics, 2000), 142–44; Samuel Eliot Morison, *The Oxford History of the American People* (New York: Oxford University Press, 1965), 936.

3. Lendol Calder, *Financing the American Dream: A Cultural History of Consumer Credit* (Princeton: Princeton University Press, 1999), 3–203.

4. Ibid., 198.

5. John Caples, *Tested Advertising Methods*, 5th ed. (Paramus: Prentice-Hall, 1997); Leuchtenburg, *Perils of Prosperity*, 242.

6. Allen, *Only Yesterday*, 141.

7. Calder, *Financing the American Dream*, 201.

8. *Historical Statistics of the United States*, 2:989; U.S. Department of Commerce, Bureau of Economic Analysis, National Income and Product Accounts (available at www.bea.doc.gov).

9. That is, mortgages for one- to four-family homes. *Historical Statistics of the United States*, 2:989; U.S. Department of Commerce, Bureau of Economic Analysis, National Income and Product Accounts.

10. Jean-Baptiste Say, *A Treatise on Political Economy*, Reprints of Economic Classics (New York: Augustus M. Kelley, 1971), 130; John Maynard Keynes, *The General Theory of Employment, Interest, and Money* (New York: Harcourt Brace, 1936), 18–26.

11. Andrew W. Mellon, *Taxation: The People's Business* (New York: Macmillan, 1924), 12.

12. Leuchtenburg, *Perils of Prosperity*, 190, 189, 99; *Historical Statistics of the United States*, 1:178.

13. *Historical Statistics of the United States*, 1:162, 1:170, 1:302, 1:301.

14. Burton G. Malkiel, *A Random Walk Down Wall Street* (New York: W. W. Norton, 1999), 46–53.

15. William E. Leuchtenburg, *Franklin Roosevelt and the New Deal* (New York: Harper Torchbooks, 1963), 60.

16. Ibid., 1–3; for unemployment estimate, see *Historical Statistics of the United States*, 1:135.

17. Peter Temin, *Did Monetary Forces Cause the Great Depression?* (New York: W. W. Norton, 1976).

18. *Historical Statistics of the United States,* 2:716, 2:618.

19. Ibid., 1:224; White House, Office of Management and Budget, *Historical Tables: Budget of the United States: Fiscal Year 2006* (Washington, D.C.: GPO, 2005), 21–22.

20. Later official estimates of unemployment by the Bureau of Labor Statistics, based on work by the scholar Stanley Lebergott, placed unemployment in 1942 at 4.7 percent. However, these estimates treated workers employed in federal public works programs as unemployed. When public works workers are treated as employed, the estimate is reduced from 4.7 to 3.1 percent. See Michael R. Darby, "Three-and-a-Half Million U.S. Employees Have Been Mislaid: Or, an Explanation for Unemployment, 1934–1941," *Journal of Political Economy* 84, no. 1 (1976): 8, and also discussion in chapter 6 below.

21. See Peter Temin, *Lessons from the Great Depression* (Cambridge: MIT Press, 1990).

22. The centrality of monetary policy as a cause of the Great Depression was first argued by Milton Friedman and Anna Jacobson Schwartz, *A Monetary History of the United States 1867–1960* (Princeton: Princeton University Press, 1963), 299–419.

23. Leuchtenburg, *Perils of Prosperity,* 250.

24. U.S. Department of Commerce, *Statistical Abstract of the United States 1936* (Washington, D.C.: GPO, 1936), 252.

25. *Historical Statistics of the United States,* 2:992.

26. Leuchtenburg, *Perils of Prosperity,* 255–56.

Chapter 6.
The Renewal of the American Dream

1. William E. Leuchtenburg, *Franklin Roosevelt and the New Deal* (New York: Harper Torchbooks, 1963), 11.

2. Arthur M. Schlesinger, Jr., "The 'Hundred Days' of F.D.R.," *New York Times,* April 10, 1983.

3. Frances Perkins, *The Roosevelt I Knew* (New York: Viking, 1946), 225–26.

4. Leuchtenburg, *Franklin Roosevelt,* 51.

5. U.S. Department of Commerce, *Statistical Abstract of the United States 1936* (Washington, D.C.: GPO, 1936), 232; National Bureau of Economic Re-

search, "Business Cycles Expansions and Contractions"; available at http://www.nber.org/cycles.html/; *Historical Statistics of the United States*, 2:992.

6. See Federal Reserve Bank historical data on federal funds rate at http://www.federalreserve.gov/releases/H15/data/m/fedfund.txt.

7. White House, Office of Management and Budget, *Historical Tables: Budget of the United States: Fiscal Year 2006* (Washington, D.C.: GPO, 2005), 21–22; *Historical Statistics of the United States*, 1:224.

8. Jeremy Atack and Peter Passell, *A New Economic View of American History*, 2d ed. (New York: W. W. Norton, 1979), 639–40.

9. White House, Office of Management and Budget, *Historical Tables: Budget of the United States: Fiscal Year 2006* (Washington, D.C.: GPO, 2005), 21–22; *Historical Statistics of the United States*, 1:224.

10. Michael R. Darby, "Three-and-a-Half Million U.S. Employees Have Been Mislaid: Or, an Explanation for Unemployment, 1934–1941," *Journal of Political Economy* 84, no. 1 (1976): 1–16. Cf. Atack and Passell, *A New Economic View of American History*, 626–31.

11. Leuchtenburg, *Franklin Roosevelt*, 150–52.

12. Darby, "Three-and-a-Half Million U.S. Employees," 8.

13. Franklin D. Roosevelt, "State of the Union Address," January 11, 1944.

14. *Historical Statistics of the United States*, 2:1147.

15. Ibid.

16. G. J. Santoni, "The Employment Act of 1946: Some History Notes," *Federal Reserve Bank of St. Louis Review* (March 1986): 5–16.

17. Stephen E. Ambrose, *Eisenhower*, vol. 2, *The President* (New York: Simon and Schuster, 1984), 251, 326, 459–50.

18. *Historical Statistics of the United States*, 1:224; White House, Office of Management and Budget, *Historical Tables: Budget of the United States: Fiscal Year 2006* (Washington, D.C.: GPO, 2005), 21–22.

19. *Historical Statistics of the United States*, 1:135.

20. Ibid., 1:169–70, 1:302.

21. National Bureau of Economic Research, "Business Cycles Expansions and Contractions"; available at http://www.nber.org/cycles.html/; *Historical Statistics of the United States*, 1:135

22. *Historical Tables: Budget of the United States*, 21–22, 46–47; *Historical Statistics of the United States*, 1:224.

23. "The New Doctrinarianism," *New York Times*, October 21, 1954, 6.

24. U.S. Department of Commerce, Bureau of Economic Analysis, National Income and Product Accounts; U.S. Department of Labor, Bureau of Labor Statistics. Estimates for poverty in the pre-1960s era were developed

by James Tobin. See Herbert Stein, *Presidential Economics* (Washington, D.C.: American Enterprise Institute, 1988), 427n.

25. A. W. H. Phillips, "The Relation between Unemployment and the Rate of Change of Money Wage Rates in the United Kingdom, 1861–1957," *Economica* n.s. 25, no. 100 (1958): 283–99.

26. Paul A. Samuelson and Robert M. Solow, "Analytical Aspects of Anti-Inflation Policy," *American Economic Review* 50, no. 2 (1960): 177–94.

27. Arthur M. Schlesinger, Jr., *A Thousand Days* (Boston: Houghton Mifflin, 1965), 641–48.

28. Robert E. Thompson, "Heller's Concepts Now Prevail," *Washington Post, Times Herald*, February 18, 1963, A5.

29. John F. Kennedy, "State of the Union Address," January 30, 1961; John F. Kennedy, "State of the Union Address," January 11, 1962.

30. John F. Kennedy, "Commencement Address at Yale University," June 11, 1962.

31. Bernard D. Nossiter, "Taxes to Be Reduced If Recovery Falters," *Washington Post, Times Herald*, June 7, 1962, A1; Bernard D. Nossiter, "Kennedy Sees Tax Cut Stimulating Economy," *Washington Post, Times Herald*, June 8, 1962, A1; "Case and Goldwater Urge Tax Cuts Now," *Washington Post, Times Herald*, July 15, 1962, A13; Bernard D. Nossiter, "Job Figures Dim Hope for Tax Cut; Kennedy Indicates Reduction Request Unlikely This Year," *Washington Post, Times Herald* August 2, 1962, A1.

32. Carroll Kirkpatrick, "Kennedy Puts Tax Cut at Top of His List for 1963 Legislation," *Washington Post, Times Herald*, January 3, 1963, A1; Joseph A. Loftus, "Economy Viewed in Human Way in Report by Kennedy Advisers," *New York Times*, January 23, 1962, 15; Thompson, "Heller's Concepts Now Prevail."

33. U.S. Department of Commerce, Bureau of Economic Analysis, National Income and Product Accounts; U.S. Department of Labor, Bureau of Labor Statistics.

34. "The Economic Report," *Washington Post, Times Herald*, January 28, 1966, A18; *Time*, December 31, 1965.

35. *Historical Tables: Budget of the United States*, 47–48; U.S. Department of Commerce, Bureau of Economic Analysis, National Income and Product Accounts.

36. Stein, *Presidential Economics*, 118–19.

37. Ibid., 120.

38. M. J. Rossant, "An Economic Schism," *New York Times*, May 4, 1966, 65.

39. Stein, *Presidential Economics*, 135.

40. U.S. Department of Labor, Bureau of Labor Statistics.

41. A. M. Okun, "Efficient Disinflationary Policies," *American Economic Review* 68, no. 2 (1978): 348–52; Stein, *Presidential Economics*, 217–18; U.S. Department of Labor, Bureau of Labor Statistics.

42. Daniel Yankelovich, "Taking Account of the Non-Economic Features of Inflation," presented to American Council of Life Insurance, February 1979, cited in Robert J. Samuelson, "Unsung Triumph," *Washington Post*, June 9, 2004, A21.

43. Milton Friedman and Anna Jacobson Schwartz, *A Monetary History of the United States 1867–1960* (Princeton: Princeton University Press, 1963).

44. Milton Friedman, "The Role of Monetary Policy," *American Economic Review* 58 (March 1968): 1–17.

Chapter 7.
The New Gospel of Wealth

1. Bruce Bartlett, *Reaganomics: Supply-Side Economics in Action* (New York: Quill, 1982), 1.

2. Herbert Stein, *Presidential Economics* (Washington, D.C.: American Enterprise Institute, 1988), 239.

3. Cited in ibid., 3–4.

4. Irving Kristol, "American Conservatism 1945–1995," *The Public Interest*, no. 121 (Fall 1995).

5. Stein, *Presidential Economics*, 236, 255–57.

6. Ibid., 237–49.

7. Leonard Silk, "Trying to Repeal Keynes," *New York Times*, February 20, 1981.

8. Stein, *Presidential Economics*, 259.

9. Lou Cannon, *Reagan* (New York: Perigree, 1982), 91–97; see texts of Reagan's 1957 Eureka College Commencement Address and 1964 speech "A Time for Choosing," at http://65.126.3.86/reagan/html/reagan_speeches.shtml; Haynes Johnson, "Resurrection of Coolidge—The Stamping of Nostalgia's Clay Feet," *Washington Post*, June 7, 1981, A3.

10. Cannon, *Reagan*, 235–37; see, for example, Rowland Evans and Robert Novak, "Reagan's Social Security Gaffe," *Washington Post*, December 20, 1975, A17.

11. Cited in Stein, *Presidential Economics*, 256.

12. Ronald Reagan, "Inaugural Address," January 20, 1981; Leonard

Silk, "Major Change in Theory Seen," *New York Times,* March 5, 1980, D2; Silk, "Trying to Repeal Keynes."

13. U.S. Department of Commerce, Bureau of Economic Analysis, National Income and Product Accounts; U.S. Department of Labor, Bureau of Labor Statistics.

14. See, for example, Jack F. Kemp, "New York State's (Groan) Taxes," May 20, 1978, 19.

15. For a detailed discussion of this literature, see chapter 8.

16. See, for example, White House, *Economic Report of the President 1996* (Washington, D.C.: GPO, 1996), 18–21.

17. George W. Bush, "President's Remarks to the Latino Coalition," February 26, 2003; George W. Bush, "Remarks by the President to Women Business Leaders," March 1, 2001.

18. Cited in William Greider, "Rolling Back the Twentieth Century," *The Nation,* May 12, 2003.

19. Alan Greenspan and James Kennedy, "Estimates of Home Mortgage Originations, Repayments, and Debt On One-to-Four-Family Residences," Working Paper 2005–41 (Washington, D.C.: Board of Governors of the Federal Reserve, 2005); William G. Gale and Peter R. Orszag, "Bush Administration Tax Policy: Short-Term Stimulus," *Tax Notes* (Tax Policy Center), November 1, 2004. The short-term stimulus effect of either home equity cash-outs or tax cuts depends on how much of the money consumers choose to spend. Estimates of this "marginal propensity to consume" (MPC) vary and are difficult to make precise. A Fed study based on surveys of homeowners who cashed out home equity in 2000 and 2001 estimated that homeowners spent 16 percent of the money on consumer goods and ploughed another 35 percent into home improvement—i.e., returning 51 percent to the economy in the form of consumption or residential investment spending. A separate Fed study of taxpayers' propensity to spend the reduced withholding and child credit allowances under the Bush 2003 tax cuts estimated the MPC at approximately 25 percent, but acknowledged it could be significantly higher. Since these MPC estimates are known to be slippery, I have simply cited the total cash amounts for equity cash-outs and tax cuts. See Margaret M. McConnell, Richard W. Peach, and Alex Al-Haschimi, "After the Refinancing Boom: Will Consumers Scale Back Their Spending?" *Current Issues in Economics and Finance* (Federal Reserve Bank of New York) 9, no. 12 (December 2003), and Julia Lynn Coronado, Joseph P. Lupton, and Louise M. Sheiner, "The Household Spending Response to the 2003 Tax Cut: Evidence from Survey Data," Working Paper 2005–32 (Washington, D.C.: Board of Governors of the Federal Reserve Bank, 2005).

Chapter 8.
The Current Debate

1. The basic findings of this chapter are presented in greater detail in Norton Garfinkle, "Supply-Side vs. Demand-Side Tax Cuts and U.S. Economic Growth 1951–2004," *Critical Review* 17, nos. 3–4 (2005). www.criticalreview.com.

2. R. Glenn Hubbard, "Testimony before U.S. Congress Joint Economic Committee," May 23, 2001.

3. George W. Bush, "Remarks by the President at Electronic Industries Alliance Government Industry Dinner," May 8, 2000; George W. Bush, "Remarks by the President at Chicago Mercantile Exchange," March 6, 2001; George W. Bush, "President Welcomes Treasury Secretary John Snow to Cabinet: Remarks by the President at the Swearing-In Ceremony for Treasury Secretary John Snow, The Cash Room, The Treasury Building," February 7, 2003.

4. William G. Gale and Samara R. Potter, "An Economic Evaluation of the Economic Growth and Tax Relief Reconciliation Act of 2001," *National Tax Journal* 15, no. 1 (2002): 133–86; Martin Feldstein, "Budget Deficits, Tax Rules, and Real Interest Rates," Working Paper no. 1970 (Cambridge, Mass.: National Bureau of Economic Research, 1986); Martin Feldstein and Douglas W. Elmendorf, "Budget Deficits, Tax Incentives, and Inflation: A Surprising Lesson from the 1983–1984 Recovery," Working Paper no. 2819 (Cambridge, Mass.: National Bureau of Economic Research, 1989); Martin Feldstein and Douglas W. Elmendorf, "Budget Deficits, Tax Incentives, and Inflation: A Surprising Lesson from the 1983–1984 Recovery," in Lawrence H. Summers, ed., *Tax Policy and the Economy* (Cambridge, Mass.: National Bureau of Economic Research, 1989), 3:1–23.

5. Eric Engen and Jonathan Skinner, "Taxation and Economic Growth," *National Tax Journal* 49, no. 4 (1996): 617–42. Harvey S. Rosen, "The Case for Making the Tax Cuts Permanent." White House, May 10, 2004 (available at http://www.whitehouse.gov/cea/nta-spring.html); R. Glenn Hubbard, "The Second-Term Economy," *Wall Street Journal,* November 9, 2004.

6. Tax Policy Center, "EGTRRA, JCWA, and JGTRRA: Distribution of Individual Income, Corporate, and Estate Tax Change by Cash Income Class, 2004," Table T04–0051, 2004 (available at http://www.taxpolicycenter.org/TaxModel/tmdb/TMTemplate.cfm?DocID=625&topic2ID=40&topic3ID=81&DocTypeID=1).

7. Robert Carroll, Douglas Holtz-Eakin, Mark Rider, and Harvey S. Rosen, "Entrepreneurs, Income Taxes, and Investment," in Joel Slemrod, ed.,

Does Atlas Shrug? The Economic Consequences of Taxing the Rich (Cambridge: Harvard University Press, 2000), 427–55; Robert Carroll, Douglas Holtz-Eakin, Mark Rider, and Harvey S. Rosen, "Income Taxes and Entrepreneurs' Use of Labor," *Journal of Labor Economics* 18, no. 2 (2000): 324–51; Robert Carroll, Douglas Holtz-Eakin, Mark Rider, and Harvey S. Rosen, "Personal Income Taxes and the Growth of Small Firms," in James Poterba, ed., *Tax Policy and the Economy* (Cambridge: MIT Press, 2001), 15: 121–46.

8. Rosen, "The Case for Making the Tax Cuts Permanent"; Hubbard, "Testimony before U.S. Congress Joint Economic Committee."

9. Sources for data are as follows: GDP growth, growth in real personal consumption expenditures, real business investment growth (real growth in gross nonresidential fixed investment): U.S. Department of Commerce, Bureau of Economic Analysis, National Income and Product Accounts. Employment growth and unemployment rate: U.S. Department of Labor, Bureau of Labor Statistics. Top marginal income tax rates: Tax Policy Center. For each statistical series, I classified the fifty-four years into three eighteen-year groups described as "best," "middle," and "worst" performance levels. See appendix.

10. Figures for gross nonresidential fixed investment provide a better index of the behavioral effect of tax policy changes than the net figures, which include depreciation. Gross figures reflect the actual amount of money invested in businesses in a given year.

11. James Tobin, "Monetary Policy," in David R. Henderson, ed., *The Concise Encyclopedia of Economics* (2001) (available at http://www.econlib .org/library/Enc/MonetaryPolicy.html).

12. Economic Policy Institute, "Economists' Statement" (2001) (available at http://www.epinet.org/press_releases/economiststatement042001.pdf).

13. White House, *Economic Report of the President* (Washington, D.C.: GPO, 2002).

14. Peter R. Orszag, "The Bush Tax Cut Is Now about the Same Size as the Reagan Tax Cuts," Center on Budget and Policy Priorities (2001) (available at http://www.cbpp.org/4–19–01tax.htm).

15. Congressional Budget Office, *The Changing Distribution of Federal Taxes: A Closer Look at 1980*. Tax Policy Center, "EGTRRA, JCWA, and JGTRRA: Distribution of Individual Income, Corporate, and Estate Tax Change by Cash Income Class, 2004," Table T04–0051 (2004) (available at http://www .taxpolicycenter.org/TaxModel/tmdb/TMTemplate.cfm?DocID=625&topic2ID =40&topic3ID=81&DocTypeID=1).

16. The growth in investment in 2004 can best be understood as a response to the Bush administration's 2004 one-year 50 percent "bonus depre-

ciation" tax deduction for all business investment by corporations and individuals. Corporate taxpaying entities that account for roughly 90 percent of all business investment in the economy were primarily responsible for the high rate of business investment in 2004. It would be hard to attribute this investment level to a response by pass-through business owners to the 2003 reduction in the top marginal personal income tax rate since these business owners account for only 10 percent of all business investment.

17. Commission on Presidential Debates, "The First Gore–Bush Presidential Debate," October 3, 2000, unofficial transcript (available at http://www.debates.org/pages/trans2000a.html); "The President's News Conference in Crawford, Texas," *Weekly Compilation of Presidential Documents* 37, no. 34 (27 August 2001): 1209–18.

18. See Gale and Potter, "An Economic Evaluation of the Economic Growth and Tax Relief Reconciliation Act of 2001."

19. Employment during the period under study is best measured by growth in employment rather than by the unemployment rate. Employment growth is a directly measurable statistic. By contrast, the unemployment rate is derived by dividing the number of people employed by the number classified as being in the workforce (i.e., employed or "looking for work"). The unemployment rate can be an unreliable statistic. The number of people working or available for work can be misclassified as in the statistics for the Depression years or can be substantially affected by a change in the number of people who temporarily or permanently enter or drop out of the workforce. In some cases, such as the relatively weak economic period of January 2001–March 2006, the unemployment rate declined while employment growth was only 38,000 per month, substantially less than the 150,000 per month required to provide jobs for new entrants to the workforce. The anomaly can best be understood as a result of people dropping out of the workforce due to a decline in the number of available jobs. By contrast, in the relatively strong economic period 1993–2000 employment growth was substantially higher (240,000 per month) as new people entered the workforce in response to an increase in the number of available jobs.

Chapter 9.
The Way Forward

1. Robert H. Frank and Philip J. Cook, *The Winner-Take-All Society* (New York: Free Press, 1995).

Index

224

Index

economic vision: economic growth,
4–5; future directions, 196–200;
laissez-faire economics, 14–15, 17,
52–67, 88, 96, 144–45; Lincolnian
ideal, 13–15, 27–30, 36–39, 43–46;
middle-class ideal, 12–13, 37–39;
Republican Party, 43–44; Roosevelt
administration, 16–17; scientific
approach, 52–57; trickle-down
economics, 73, 94–95, 156. *See also*
demand-side economics; progressive
tax system; regressive tax system;
supply-side economics
Eisenhower, Dwight D., 7, 122–27
electricity, 89–90
Elmendorf, Douglas, 166
Emergency Banking Act (1933), 114–15
Emerson, Ralph Waldo, 91
Employment Act (1946), 121–22
employment/unemployment: Carter
administration, 139–41, 143; consumer demand and borrowing, 178–
80; deficit spending programs,
128–29; demand-side economics,
179–88, 191; economic policy, 7, 21;
Eisenhower administration, 124–
26, 127; Great Depression, 5–6, 99–
106; growth rate, 1–3, 134, 140, 186;
and inflation rates, 128–29, 139–42;
insurance programs, 113–17, 124–26;
Kennedy administration, 131–34;
neo-Keynesian economics, 128–29,
131–35; public works programs, 114;
Reagan administration, 155; regulation legislation, 120–22; Roosevelt
administration, 108, 114, 120–22,
212n20; time-series analysis, 172–74,
177–79; top marginal income tax
rate, 172–74, 176–77, 180; World
War II, 118. *See also* unionization;
working conditions; working-class
families

Engen, Eric, 167–68, 171–72
estate taxes, 2, 71, 85, 160–61, 191
Etzioni, Amitai, 197
evolution, theory of, 57–60

factual economic consequences, 5, 10,
17–20
Fair Labor Standards Act (1938), 116
fairness, 6, 8, 21, 22–23, 193–94
Family and Medical Leave Act (1993),
158
Federal Deposit Insurance Corporation (FDIC), 115
federal expenditures: Eisenhower
administration, 123–26; Hoover
administration, 105; Johnson administration, 135–37; post–Civil
War decades, 48–49; post–World
War I decade, 103; probusiness
policies, 61–62; Reagan administration, 153; Roosevelt administration, 111, 118
Federal Housing Administration
(FHA), 115
Federal Reserve: interest rates, 7, 100,
104, 110–11, 137–38, 143, 162, 176;
monetary policy, 10, 142, 154–57,
162; regulation legislation, 115
Federal Reserve Act (1913), 85
federal surpluses, 1–2, 4, 25, 161
Federal Trade Commission (FTC), 96
Federal Trade Commission Act (1914),
85
Feldstein, Martin, 157, 166, 187
finance companies, 90–91
fiscal policy, 102–3, 109, 111–12, 143,
153, 175, 192
Fisk, James, 62
flat tax, 23
Ford, Gerald, 139, 149, 153
Ford, Henry, 95, 191–92
Frank, Robert H., 190